Di quell' a - mor, quell'a - mor chè pal-pi-to

The Little Book
of Opera

The Little Book of
Opera

⇒ *an anthology* ⇐

Edited by Duncan Bock

A Balliett & Fitzgerald Book

THE ATLANTIC MONTHLY PRESS
NEW YORK

Compilation copyright © 1996 by Balliett & Fitzgerald, Inc.
Commentary copyright © 1996 by Duncan Bock

Published simultaneously in Canada
Printed in the United States of America

First edition

Library of Congress Cataloging-in-Publication Data
    The little book of opera: an anthology / edited by Duncan Bock.—
    1st ed.
        p. cm.
    "A Balliett & Fitzgerald book."
    ISBN 0-87113-649-X
    1. Opera.   I. Bock, Duncan.
ML1700.L585 1996
782.1—dc20   96-28051
                                                    MN

Design by Susan Canavan

Series Editor: Will Balliett

The Atlantic Monthly Press
841 Broadway
New York, NY 10003

10 9 8 7 6 5 4 3 2 1

Foreword

———•◦•———

The idea for this book was inspired by my late father, Ervin Morgan Entrekin. My father was born in Atlanta, Georgia, in 1927, was educated at Vanderbilt University, and lived and practiced law in Nashville, Tennessee, until his death in 1990.

Daddy was an astute businessman who built a successful law practice. He was also quite a remarkable person—one of those rare souls who inspired almost everyone whose life he touched. To this day, when I am back home in Tennessee, I will inevitably encounter strangers who, upon hearing my name, will ask if I am Ervin Entrekin's son, and then proceed to recount some favor my father did for them, or simply remark on how highly they regarded him.

In addition to being a respected attorney, Daddy was a great lover and collector of art and had a deep and abiding passion for music, especially opera. My first introduction to opera was with my father. When I was twelve, we were on a family trip to New York, and as the oldest child, I was allowed to accompany my father to the opera. I recall being very excited, probably because I was getting to do something my siblings weren't. We went to *La Traviata* at the Met, and I think I lasted through almost the whole first act before I fell asleep. But—I had been to the opera.

After I finished college and moved to New York, it gave my parents a great excuse to come even more often to a city they loved. With my mother, Jane, Daddy would come up and go to galleries and to the art auctions in the fall and spring. But his real passion was the opera. During the opera season, they would come up from Nashville ten or twelve times. Often, they would fly up Friday, go to the opera Friday night, then to a Saturday matinee followed by the Saturday night performance. I have always loved my parents and enjoyed their company, and I wanted to see them during their frequent visits, so I began to go to the opera. I remember meeting them at the Met one night after a long day at the office. After sitting through four or five hours of a Wagner opera I said to my father, "Daddy, couldn't you start me on the shorter ones?"

So, he did. Eventually I came to look forward to going to the opera. Occasionally I would even invite a young woman to accompany me. We would meet my parents at the restaurant at the Metropolitan Opera House in Lincoln Center. Over dinner, my father, a courtly southern lawyer (think Gregory Peck as Atticus Finch in *To Kill a Mockingbird*) would tell the story of the opera we were about to see in his deep southern accent and alert us to the musical themes and key passages to look for. It made for a killer date.

A few months after my father died, I went with my mother to see Donizetti's *L'Elisir d'Amore*. In the second act, Pavarotti as Nemorino sang the famous aria "Una furtiva lagrima." As Pavarotti sang this beautiful lament of lovers parting, I was moved as only opera can move you and looked over at my mother. Tears were flowing down our cheeks as we both were thinking of the wonderful man we had known and loved and who had introduced us to opera.

I continue to go to the opera and love it more and more as the years go by. I am indebted to my father for many things (among others, he encouraged me to go out on my own as a publisher and was the primary investor in the company I started that through merger and acquisition became Grove/Atlantic, the independent publishing house that produced this book), not least among them the marvelous, excessive, wonderful art form that is opera. This book is a celebration of opera and it is dedicated to the memory of my father. Thank you, Daddy, for everything—we miss you.

E. Morgan Entrekin, Jr.
Publisher

⊰ CONTENTS ⊱

The Age of Innocence

(an excerpt from the novel)

Edith Wharton

At the opera house, intrigue in the boxes is often at least as important as what happens onstage. Wharton is a master at painting the play between public and private lives, and here she casts a satirical glance at New York society through her opera glasses.

On a January evening of the early seventies, Christine Nilsson was singing in *Faust* at the Academy of Music in New York.

Though there was already talk of the erection, in remote metropolitan distances "above the Forties," of a new Opera House which should compete in costliness and splendor with those of the great European capitals, the world of fashion was still content to reassemble every winter in the shabby red and gold boxes in the sociable old Academy. Conservatives cherished it for being small and inconvenient, and thus keeping out the "new people" whom New York was beginning to dread and yet be drawn to; and the sentimental clung to it for its historic associations, and the musical for its excellent acoustics, always so problematic a quality in halls built for the hearing of music.

It was Madame Nilsson's first appearance that winter, and what the daily press had already learned to describe as "an exceptionally brilliant audience" had gathered to hear her, transported through the slippery, snowy streets in private broughams, in the spacious family landau, or in the humbler but more convenient "Brown *coupé*." To come to the Opera in a Brown *coupé* was almost as honorable a way of arriving as in one's own carriage; and departure by the same means had the immense advantage of enabling one (with a playful allusion to democratic principles) to scramble into the first Brown conveyance in the line, instead of waiting till the cold-and-gin congested nose of one's own coachman gleamed under the portico of the Academy. It was one of the great livery-stableman's most masterly intuitions to have discovered that Americans want to get away from amusement even more quickly than they want to get to it.

When Newland Archer opened the door at the back of the club box the curtain had just gone up on the garden scene. There was no reason why the young man should not have come earlier, for he had dined at seven, alone with his mother and sister, and had lingered afterward over a cigar in the Gothic library with glazed black-walnut bookcases and finial-topped chairs which was the only room in the house where Mrs. Archer allowed smoking. But, in the first place, New York was a metropolis, and perfectly aware that in metropolises it was "not the thing" to arrive early at the opera; and what was or was not "the thing" played a part as important in Newland Archer's New York as the inscrutable totem terrors that had ruled the destinies of his forefathers thousands of years ago.

The second reason for his delay was a personal one. He had dawdled over his cigar because he was at heart a dilettante, and thinking over a pleasure to come often gave him a subtler satisfaction than its realization. This was especially the case when the pleasure was a delicate one, as his pleasures mostly were; and on this occasion the moment he looked forward to was so rare and exquisite in quality that—well, if he had timed his arrival in accord with the prima donna's stage-manager he could not have entered the Academy at a more significant moment than just as she was singing: "He loves me—he loves me not—*he loves me!*—" and sprinkling the falling daisy petals with notes clear as dew.

She sang, of course, "*M'ama!*" and not "he loves me," since an unalterable and unquestioned law of the musical world required that the German text of French operas sung by Swedish artists should be translated into Italian for the clearer understanding of English-speaking audiences. This seemed as natural to Newland Archer as all the other conventions on which his life was molded: such as the duty of using two silver-backed brushes with his

The Age of Innocence

monogram in blue enamel to part his hair, and of never appearing in society without a flower (preferably a gardenia) in his buttonhole.

"M'ama . . . non m'ama . . ." the prima donna sang, and "M'ama!," with a final burst of love triumphant, as she pressed the disheveled daisy to her lips and lifted her large eyes to the sophisticated countenance of the little brown Faust-Capoul, who was vainly trying, in a tight purple velvet doublet and plumed cap, to look as pure and true as his artless victim.

Newland Archer, leaning against the wall at the back of the club box, turned his eyes from the stage and scanned the opposite side of the house. Directly facing him was the box of old Mrs. Manson Mingott, whose monstrous obesity had long since made it impossible for her to attend the Opera, but who was always represented on fashionable nights by some of the younger members of the family. On this occasion, the front of her box was filled by her daughter-in-law, Mrs. Lovell Mingott, and her daughter, Mrs. Welland; and slightly withdrawn behind these brocaded matrons sat a young girl in white with eyes ecstatically fixed on the stagelovers. As Madame Nilsson's "M'ama!" thrilled out above the silent house (the boxes always stopped talking during the Daisy Song) a warm pink mounted to the girl's cheek, mantled her brow to the roots of her fair braids, and suffused the young slope of her breast to the line where it met a modest tulle tucker fastened with a single gardenia. She dropped her eyes to the immense bouquet of lilies-of-the-valley on her knee, and Newland Archer saw her white-gloved finger-tips touch the flowers softly. He drew a breath of satisfied vanity and his eyes returned to the stage.

No expense had been spared on the setting, which was acknowledged to be very beautiful even by people who shared his acquaintance with the Opera houses of Paris and Vienna. The foreground, to the footlights, was covered with emerald green cloth. In the middle distance symmetrical mounds of woolly green moss bounded by croquet hoops formed the base of shrubs shaped like orange-trees but studded with large pink and red roses. Gigantic pansies, considerably larger than the roses, and closely resembling the floral penwipers made by female parishioners for fashionable clergymen, sprang from the moss beneath the rosetrees; and here and there a daisy grafted on a rosebranch flowered with a luxuriance prophetic of Mr. Luther Burbank's far-off prodigies.

In the center of this enchanted garden Madame Nilsson, in white cashmere slashed with pale blue satin, a reticule dangling from a blue girdle, and large yellow braids carefully disposed on each side of her muslin chemisette, listened with downcast eyes to M. Capoul's impassioned wooing, and affected a guileless incomprehension of his designs whenever, by word or glance, he persuasively indicated the ground floor window of the neat brick villa projecting obliquely from the right wing.

"The darling!" thought Newland Archer, his glance flitting back to the young girl with the lilies-of-the-valley. "She doesn't even guess what it's all about." And he contemplated her absorbed young face with a thrill of possessorship in which pride in his own masculine initiation was mingled with a tender reverence for her abysmal purity. "We'll read Faust together . . . by the Italian lakes . . ." he thought, somewhat hazily confusing the scene of his projected honeymoon with the masterpieces of literature which it would be his manly privilege to reveal to his bride. It was only that afternoon that May Welland had let him guess that she "cared" (New York's consecrated phrase of maiden avowal), and already his imagination, leaping ahead of the engagement ring, the betrothal kiss and the march from Lohengrin, pictured her at his side in some scene of old European witchery.

He did not in the least wish the future Mrs. Newland Archer to be a simpleton. He meant her (thanks to enlightening companionship) to develop a social tact and readiness of wit enabling her to hold her own with the most popular married women of the "younger set," in which it was the recognized custom to attract masculine homage while playfully discouraging it. If he had probed to the bottom of his vanity (as he sometimes nearly did) he would have found there the wish that his wife should be as worldly-wise and as eager to please as the married lady whose charms had held his fancy through two mildly agitated years; without, of course, any hint of the frailty which had so nearly marred that unhappy being's life, and had disarranged his own plans for a whole winter.

The Age of Innocence

How this miracle of fire and ice was to be created, and to sustain itself in a harsh world, he had never taken the time to think out; but he was content to hold his view without analyzing it, since he knew it was that of all the carefully-brushed, white waistcoated, buttonhole-flowered gentlemen who succeeded each other in the club box, exchanged friendly greetings with him, and turned their opera-glasses critically on the circle of ladies who were the product of the system. In matters intellectual and artistic Newland Archer felt himself distinctly the superior of these chosen specimens of old New York gentility; he had probably read more, thought more, and even seen a good deal more of the world, than any other man of the number. Singly they betrayed their inferiority; but grouped together they represented "New York," and the habit of masculine solidarity made him accept their doctrine on all the issues called moral. He instinctively felt that in this respect it would be troublesome—and also rather bad form—to strike out for himself.

"Well—upon my soul!" exclaimed Lawrence Lefferts, turning his opera-glass abruptly away from the stage. Lawrence Lefferts was, on the whole, the foremost authority on "form" in New York. He had probably devoted more time than anyone else to the study of this intricate and fascinating question; but study alone could not account for his complete and easy competence. One had only to look at him, from the slant of his bald forehead and the curve of his beautiful fair moustache to the long patent-leather feet at the other end of his lean and elegant person, to feel that the knowledge of "form" must be congenital in anyone who knew how to wear such good clothes so carelessly and carry such height with so much lounging grace. As a young admirer had once said of him: "If anybody can tell a fellow just when to wear a black tie with evening clothes and when not to, it's Larry Lefferts." And on the question of pumps versus patent-leather "Oxfords" his authority had never been disputed.

"My God!" he said; and silently handed his glass to old Sillerton Jackson.

Newland Archer, following Lefferts's glance, saw with surprise that his exclamation had been occasioned by the entry of a new figure into old Mrs. Mingott's box. It was that of a slim young woman, a little less tall than May Welland, with brown hair growing in close curls about her temples and held in place by a narrow band of diamonds. The suggestion of this headdress, which gave her what was then called a "Josephine look," was carried out in the cut of the dark blue velvet gown rather theatrically caught up under her bosom by a girdle with a large old-fashioned clasp. The wearer of this unusual dress, who seemed quite unconscious of the attention it was attracting, stood a moment in the center of the box, discussing with Mrs. Welland the propriety of taking the latter's place in the front righthand corner; then she yielded with a slight smile, and seated herself in line with Mrs. Welland's sister-in-law, Mrs. Lovell Mingott, who was installed in the opposite corner.

Mr. Sillerton Jackson had returned the opera-glass to Lawrence Lefferts. The whole of the club turned instinctively, waiting to hear what the old man had to say; for old Mr. Jackson was as great an authority on "family" as Lawrence Lefferts was on "form." He knew all the ramifications of New York's cousinships; and could not only elucidate such complicated questions as that of the connection between the Mingotts (through the Thorleys) with the Dallases of South Carolina, and that of the relationship of the elder branch of Philadelphia Thorleys to the Albany Chiverses (on no account to be confused with the Manson Chiverses of University Place), but could also enumerate the leading characteristics of each family: as, for instance, the fabulous stinginess of the younger lines of Leffertses (the Long Island ones); or the fatal tendency of the Rushworths to make foolish matches; or the insanity recurring in every second generation of the Albany Chiverses, with whom their New York cousins had always refused to intermarry—with the disastrous exception of poor Medora Manson, who, as everybody knew . . . but then her mother was a Rushworth.

In addition to this forest of family trees, Mr. Sillerton Jackson carried between his narrow hollow temples, and under his soft thatch of silver hair, a register of most of the scandals and mysteries that had smoldered under the unruffled surface of New York society within the last fifty years. So far indeed did his information extend, and so acutely retentive was his memory, that he was supposed to be the only man who could have told you who Julius Beaufort, the banker, really was, and what had become of handsome Bob Spicer, old Mrs. Manson Mingott's

The Age of Innocence

father, who had disappeared so mysteriously (with a large sum of trust money) less than a year after his marriage, on the very day that a beautiful Spanish dancer who had been delighting thronged audiences in the old Opera-house on the Battery had taken ship for Cuba. But these mysteries, and many other, were closely locked in Mr. Jackson's breast; for not only did his keen sense of honor forbid his repeating anything privately imparted, but he was fully aware that his reputation for discretion increased his opportunities of finding out what he wanted to know.

The club box, therefore, waited in visible suspense while Mr. Sillerton Jackson handed back Lawrence Lefferts's opera-glass. For a moment he silently scrutinized the attentive group out of his filmy blue eyes overhung by old veined lids; then he gave his moustache a thoughtful twist, and said simply: "I didn't think the Mingotts would have tried it on."

Newland Archer, during this brief episode, had been thrown into a strange state of embarrassment. It was annoying that the box which was thus attracting the undivided attention of masculine New York should be that in which his betrothed was seated between her mother and aunt; and for a moment he could not identify the lady in the Empire dress, nor imagine why her presence created such excitement among the initiated. Then light dawned on him, and with it came a momentary rush of indignation. No, indeed; no one would have thought the Mingotts would have tried it on!

But they had; they undoubtably had; for the low-toned comments behind him left no doubt in Archer's mind that the young woman was May Welland's cousin, the cousin always referred to in the family as "poor Ellen Olenska." Archer knew that she had suddenly arrived from Europe a day or two previously; he had even heard from Miss Welland (not disapprovingly) that she had been to see poor Ellen, who was staying with old Mrs. Mingott. Archer entirely approved of family solidarity, and one of the qualities he most admired in the Mingotts was their resolute championship of the few black sheep that their blameless stock had produced. There was nothing mean or ungenerous in the young man's heart, and he was glad that his future wife should not be restrained by false prudery from being kind (in private) to her unhappy cousin; but to receive Countess Olenska in the family circle was a different thing from producing her in public, at the Opera of all places, and in the very box with the young girl whose engagement to him, Newland Archer, was to be announced within a few weeks. No, he felt as old Sillerton Jackson felt; he did not think the Mingotts would have tried it on!

He knew, of course, that whatever man dared (within Fifth Avenue's limits) that old Mrs. Manson Mingott, the Matriarch of the line, would dare. He had always admired the high and mighty old lady, who, in spite of having been only Catherine Spicer of Staten Island, with a father mysteriously discredited, and neither money nor position enough to make people forget it, had allied herself with the head of the wealthy Mingott line, married two of her daughters to "foreigners" (an Italian marquis and an English banker), and put the crowning touch to her audacities by building a large house of pale cream-colored stone (when brown sandstone seemed as much the only wear as a frock-coat in the afternoon) in an inaccessible wilderness near the Central Park.

Old Mrs. Mingott's foreign daughters had become a legend. They never came back to see their mother, and the latter being, like many persons of active mind and dominating will, sedentary and corpulent in her habit, had philosophically remained at home. But the cream-colored house (supposed to be modeled on the private hotels of the Parisian aristocracy) was there as a visible proof of her moral courage; and she throned in it, among pre-Revolutionary furniture and souvenirs of the Tuileries of Louis Napoleon (where she had shone in her middle age), as placidly as if there were nothing peculiar in living above Thirty-fourth Street, or in having French windows that opened like doors instead of having sashes that pushed up.

Everyone (including Mr. Sillerton Jackson) was agreed that old Catherine had never had beauty—a gift which, in the eyes of New York, justified every success, and excused a certain number of failings. Unkind people said that, like her Imperial namesake, she had won her way to success by strength of will and hardness of heart, and a kind of haughty effrontery that was somehow justified by the extreme decency and dignity of her private life. Mr. Manson Mingott

The Age of Innocence

had died when she was only twenty-eight, and had "tied up" the money with an additional caution born of the general distrust of the Spicers; but his bold young widow went her way fearlessly, mingled freely in foreign society, married her daughters in heaven knew what corrupt and fashionable circles, hobnobbed with Dukes and Ambassadors, associated familiarly with Papists, entertained Opera singers, and was the intimate friend of Mme. Taglioni; and all the while (as Sillerton Jackson was the first to proclaim) there had never been a breath on her reputation; the only respect, he always added, in which she differed from the earlier Catherine.

Mrs. Manson Mingott had long since succeeded in untying her husband's fortune, and had lived in affluence for half a century; but memories of her early straits had made her excessively thrifty, and though, when she bought a dress or a piece of furniture, she took care that it should be of the best, she could not bring herself to spend much on the transient pleasures of the table. Therefore, for totally different reasons, her food was as poor as Mrs. Archer's, and her wines did nothing to redeem it. Her relatives considered that the penury of her table discredited the Mingott name, which had always been associated with good living; but people continued to come to her in spite of the "made dishes" and flat champagne, and in reply to the remonstrances of her son Lovell (who tried to retrieve the family credit by having the best *chef* in New York) she used to say laughingly: "What's the use of two good cooks in one family, now that I've married the girls and can't eat sauces?"

Newland Archer, as he mused on these things, had once more turned his eyes toward the Mingott box. He saw that Mrs. Welland and her sister-in-law were facing their semicircle of critics with the Mingottian *aplomb* which old Catherine had inculcated in all her tribe, and that only May Welland betrayed, by a heightened color (perhaps due to the knowledge that he was watching her) a sense of the gravity of the situation. As for the cause of the commotion, she sat gracefully in her corner of the box, her eyes fixed on the stage, and revealing, as she leaned forward, a little more shoulder and bosom than New York was accustomed to seeing, at least in ladies who had reasons for wishing to pass unnoticed.

Few things seemed to Newland Archer more awful than an offense against "Taste," that far-off divinity of whom "Form" was the mere visible representative and vicegerent. Madame Olenska's pale and serious face appealed to his fancy as suited to the occasion and to her unhappy situation; but the way her dress (which had no tucker) sloped away from her thin shoulders shocked and troubled him. He hated to think of May Welland's being exposed to the influence of a young woman so careless of the dictates of Taste.

"After all," he heard one of the younger men begin behind him (everybody talked through the Mephistopheles-and-Martha scenes), "after all, just *what* happened?"

"Well—she left him; nobody attempts to deny that."

"He's an awful brute, isn't he?" continued the young enquirer, a candid Thorley, who was evidently preparing to enter the lists as the lady's champion.

"The very worst; I knew him at Nice," said Lawrence Lefferts with authority. "A half-paralyzed white sneering fellow—rather handsome head, but eyes with a lot of lashes. Well, I'll tell you the sort: when he wasn't with women he was collecting china. Paying any price for both, I understand."

There was a general laugh, and the young champion said: "Well, then—?"

"Well, then; she bolted with his secretary."

"Oh, I see." The champion's face fell.

"It didn't last long, though: I heard of her a few months later living alone in Venice. I believe Lovell Mingott went out to get her. He said she was desperately unhappy. That's all right—but this parading her at the Opera's another thing."

"Perhaps," young Thorley hazarded, "she's too unhappy to be left at home."

This was greeted with an irreverent laugh, and the youth blushed deeply, and tried to look as if he had meant to insinuate what knowing people called a "*double entendre.*"

"Well—it's queer to have brought Miss Welland, anyhow," someone said in a low tone, with a side-glance at Archer.

"Oh, that's part of the campaign: Granny's orders, no doubt," Lefferts laughed. "When the old lady does a thing she does it thoroughly."

The Age of Innocence

The act was ending, and there was a general stir in the box. Suddenly Newland Archer felt himself impelled to decisive action. The desire to be the first man to enter Mrs. Mingott's box, to proclaim to the waiting world his engagement to May Welland, and to see her through whatever difficulties her cousin's anomalous situation might involve her in; this impulse had abruptly overruled all scruples and hesitations, and sent him hurrying through the red corridors to the farther side of the house.

As he entered the box his eyes met Miss Welland's, and he saw that she had instantly understood his motive, though the family dignity which both considered so high a virtue would not permit her to tell him so. The persons of their world lived in an atmosphere of faint implications and pale delicacies, and the fact that he and she understood each other without a word seemed to the young man to bring them nearer than any explanation would have done. Her eyes said: "You see why Mamma brought me," and his answered: "I would not for the world have had you stay away."

"You know my niece Countess Olenska?" Mrs. Welland enquired as she shook hands with her future son-in-law. Archer bowed without extending his hand, as was the custom on being introduced to a lady; and Ellen Olenska bent her head slightly, keeping her own pale-gloved hands clasped on her huge fan of eagle feathers. Having greeted Mrs. Lovell Mingott, a large blond lady in creaking satin, he sat down beside his betrothed, and said in a low tone: "I hope you've told Madame Olenska that we're engaged? I want everybody to know—I want you to let me announce it this evening at the ball."

Miss Welland's face grew rosy as the dawn, and she looked at him with radiant eyes. "If you can persuade Mamma," she said; "but why should we change what is already settled?" He made no answer but that which his eyes returned, and she added, still more confidently smiling: "Tell my cousin yourself: I give you leave. She says she used to play with you when you were children."

She made way for him by pushing back her chair, and promptly, and a little ostentatiously, with the desire that the whole house should see what he was doing, Archer seated himself at the Countess Olenska's side.

"We *did* used to play together, didn't we?" she asked, turning her grave eyes to his. "You were a horrid boy, and kissed me once behind a door; but it was your cousin Vandie Newland, who never looked at me, that I was in love with." Her glance swept the horseshoe curve of boxes. "Ah, how this brings it all back to me—I see everybody here in knickerbockers and pantalettes," she said, with her trailing slightly foreign accent, her eyes returning to his face.

Agreeable as their expression was, the young man was shocked that they should reflect so unseemly a picture of the august tribunal before which, at that very moment, her case was being tried. Nothing could be in worse taste than misplaced flippancy; and he answered somewhat stiffly: "Yes, you have been away a very long time."

"Oh, centuries and centuries; so long," she said, "that I'm sure I'm dead and buried, and this dear old place is heaven," which, for reasons he could not define, struck Newland Archer as an even more disrespectful way of describing New York society.

Master
Class

(an excerpt from Act II of the play)

Terrence McNally

And who was the greatest diva of them all? In a fitting tribute to Maria Callas, McNally uses one of La Divina's Juilliard master classes to show how a great artist gets beyond the notes.

*S*omeone has placed a bouquet of flowers on the piano.

    The ACCOMPANIST *enters and sits quietly at the piano. . . .*

The house lights are lowered. There is a long wait.

Eventually, MARIA *enters. She comes to the stage apron.*

MARIA: That's better. Eh? Isn't that better? With the lights like this? Eh? It's better we don't see you up here. That's how it is in the theater. Just us and the music. Or that's how it should be. I know some singers, oh, yes, who look out at the audience, if you can imagine such a thing, when they're meant to be involved in a dramatic situation. Of course, I don't consider these people serious artists. *Pas du tout, n'est-ce que pas?* They're more like . . . oh what's the word? . . . you know, help me: no arms or legs, they swim, throw them a fish and they—seals! That's what they are: performing seals! Excuse me?

(She cups her ear to hear someone in the audience.)

    No. Absolutely not.

        So. Where were we? Did you have a good interval? I had a friend, who shall remain nameless, who used to say his favorite part of the opera was the intervals. Well, people like that, we're not going to concern ourselves with them today, thank God. To think there are actually people to whom beauty, art, what we do, isn't important! Don't get me wrong: I think we should be paid for what we do, and some of us are paid very well (it's no secret I was paid more than any of my rivals, which was the newspapers' word for them, not mine. As if I had any! How can you have rivals when no one else can do what you do?). So much has been written about it, so much nonsense. The point I'm making, and it's a very simple one, is that art is beauty and you should be paid for it. Am I making myself clear? Never give anything away. There's no more where it came from. We give the audience everything and when it's gone, *c'est ça, c'est tout. Basta, finito.* We're the ones who end up empty. "Ho dato tutto a te." Medea sings that to Jason when she learns he's abandoning her for another woman. A younger woman. A woman of importance. A princess. "Ho dato tutto a te." "I gave everything for you. Everything." That's what we artists do for people. Where would you be without us? Eh? Think about that. Just think about it while you're counting your millions or leading your boring lives with your boring wives.

(*To the* ACCOMPANIST:) Am I right?

ACCOMPANIST: I'm sorry?

MARIA: He knows I'm right.

And the friend who shall remain nameless who preferred the intervals of *Norma* to *Norma* itself was no friend. I don't know the proper word for people who are everywhere in our lives but don't wish us well at all, as it turns out. Eh? Do you know what I'm talking about? She knows what I'm talking about. I know *one* word, but I think the ceiling would fall down if I used it in this holy place, and I do believe we are in a holy place. The stage, the theater are sacred places, oh, yes. I lose my sense of humor the moment I walk through the stage door. I'm rambling. I had a terrible interval, actually. Well, you're not interested in my problems. Any more than I'm interested in yours.

Master Class

We're here to work. Put everything behind us. Am I right?

ACCOMPANIST: Absolutely.

MARIA: Don't tell me . . . it's a Jewish name, I remember that much . . . I remember the red sweater . . . *Po, po, po!* . . . I give up.

ACCOMPANIST: Weinstock—Manny Weinstock.

MARIA: Of course it is! *Siete pronto, Signor Weinstock?*

ACCOMPANIST: *Sì.*

MARIA: *Bravo, bravo, arcibravo!* You're doing very well.

ACCOMPANIST: Thank you.

MARIA: Isn't he doing well? I salute you.

(*She applauds him*)

We all salute you.

(*She encourages the audience to applaud him, then looks at the index cards she has been carrying.*)

Who's next? Lady Macbeth, Tosca, Lucia. I must say, what these students lack in voice and technique, they make up for in self-confidence. Don't laugh. That's important. Well, we shall see what we shall see. I wish them well. Next victim! That was a joke. My last one, I promise.

(*To the* ACCOMPANIST:) And what is that folderol on the piano there, please?

ACCOMPANIST: You mean the flowers? They're for you. You have an unknown admirer. Very operatic.

MARIA: Is this a classroom or a circus?

(ANOTHER SOPRANO *is coming out onto the stage. She is in an evening gown.*)

That was very naughty of someone. I won't pretend I'm not flattered, but I'm also not amused. Very, very naughty.

(*To the* SOPRANO:) *Avanti, avanti!* Don't linger. If you're going to enter, enter. If you don't want to be out here, go away. Don't giggle out there. Don't mind them, dear, I'll be right with you. Are you going somewhere after this?

SOPRANO: No.

MARIA: (*reading the card that accompanied the flowers*) "Brava, La Divina. We love you." "La Divina." Don't make me laugh. And it's always "We love you," never "*I* love you." So. Now who have we here?

SOPRANO: Sharon Graham.

MARIA: Sharon Graham. Definitely not Greek.

ACCOMPANIST: No.

MARIA: What's in a name, eh? I was Maria Meneghini Callas for a long time. Of course, I was Signora Meneghini for a time as well. So. Sharon Graham. What are you going to sing for us?

SOPRANO: Lady Macbeth?

MARIA: Are you sure you want to do that, Sharon?

SOPRANO: I also have Queen of the Night, "Der Hölle Rache" and Norma, the "Casta diva."

MARIA: I think we'll stay with Lady Macbeth. The Sleepwalking Scene, I suppose.

SOPRANO: No, "Vieni! t'affretta," I thought.

MARIA: Ah, the Letter Scene! Well, that's something. They usually all want to start with the Sleepwalking Scene. You're humble, like me, that's good. So. This is her entrance aria, yes?

SOPRANO: Yes.

MARIA: So what are you doing out here? Go away. We don't want to see you yet.

SOPRANO: You want me to go off and come back out?

MARIA: No, I want you to enter. You're on a stage. Use it. Own it. This is opera, not a voice recital. Anyone can stand there and sing. An artist enters and *is*.

SOPRANO: I thought this was a classroom.

MARIA: It doesn't matter. Never miss an opportunity to theatricalize. Astonish us, Sharon.

SOPRANO: How do I do that?

MARIA: You can start by not entering as Sharon Graham. Enter as Lady Macbeth. Enter as

Shakespeare's Lady Macbeth. Enter as Verdi's Lady Macbeth.

SOPRANO: I'll do my best.

MARIA: And Sharon, may I say one more thing? That's a beautiful gown, obviously. We've all been admiring it. It's gorgeous. I wish I had one like it.

SOPRANO: Thank you.

MARIA: But don't ever wear anything like that before midnight at the earliest, and certainly not to class. We're talking about what's appropriate. This is a master class, not some Cinderella's ball. Eh? Off you go now. And come back as her. Come back as Lady.

(The SOPRANO exits.)

Sometimes we just have to say these things, eh? Am I right? I learned the hard way. I didn't have anyone to tell me these things. I auditioned for Edward Johnson at the old Met wearing a red-and-white polka-dot dress, white gloves, a blue hat with a veil, and what I later learned were known as Joan Crawford "catch me/your-F-word me" pumps. I'm sorry, but that's what they were called. I was overweight and looked like an American flag singing *Madama Butterfly*. No wonder I wasn't engaged. She'll thank me one day.

Are we ready?

(The ACCOMPANIST nods.)

I haven't heard this music in years. Even the thought of it makes the hairs on the back of my neck stand out. I guess I'm ready. Begin.

(The ACCOMPANIST *begins to play the introduction to Lady Macbeth's entrance aria.* MARIA *listens hard, making sounds along with it, rather than actually singing the notes.*)

Satanic music, don't you think? We know where this music is coming from, don't we? What part of her body? Verdi knew his Shakespeare. The curtain is flying up now. No Sharon yet. This is an interesting choice for an entrance. I was onstage at this point.

(The music stops. No sign of the SOPRANO.)

Sharon? We're all waiting. (To the audience:) Excuse me.

(She leaves the stage and comes back a moment later.)

No Sharon. She's gone. If her skin is that thin, she's not suited for this career. It's not like I said anything about her voice. I didn't even let her open her mouth.

This will make the papers. They'll have a fine time with this. "Callas Hurts Student's Feelings."

This is just what I was talking about: If you're going to stand up here, naked, and let people judge you, you can't afford to have feelings like Sharon's. A performance is a struggle. You have to win. The audience is the enemy. We have to bring you to your knees because we're right. If I'm worried about what you're thinking about me, I can't win. I beg, I cringe for your favor instead. "Ho dato tutto a te." It doesn't work that way. You have to make them beg for yours. Dominate them. "Ho dato tutto a te." Eh? Art is domination. It's making people think that for that precise moment in time there is only one way, one voice. Yours. Eh? Anyone's feelings can be hurt. Only an artist can say "Ho dato tutto a te" center stage at La Scala and even Leonard Bernstein forgets he's Leonard Bernstein and listens to you.

Next student please. Is there water? I need water.

ACCOMPANIST: Right over there. Please, let me.

MARIA: There's one advantage to being this nearsighted. You don't have to follow the conductor. How can you? You can't see him. But I never made them follow me. No, we worked together. *Insieme. Tutto insieme.* Art is collaboration, too. Domination. Collaboration. *Ecco.* If you have feelings like Sharon, hide them. It's that simple. That's what I did. Excuse me.

(She drinks as the TENOR *comes out onto the stage.)*

Avanti, avanti. You all lack presence. Look at me. I'm drinking water and I have presence. Stand straight. Let us see who you are. *Bravo!* You're a good-looking man. You have what the Italians call *bella figura.*

TENOR: Thank you.

MARIA: That wasn't a compliment. It was a statement. We're talking turkey here. A singer has to know his assets. This is a business too, after all, let's never forget that. Domination. Collaboration. Assets. What are you?

TENOR: You mean my name?

MARIA: No, I mean your voice.

TENOR: I'm a tenor. Couldn't you tell?

MARIA: A tenor. *Gran Dio*. God save us sopranos from you tenors. And that is the only tenor joke you're going to hear from me.

TENOR: People think we're stupid.

MARIA: I wonder why that is.

TENOR: I don't know.

MARIA: Actually, I love tenors. When they sing, it's our chance to go to our dressing rooms and catch our breath. But no such luck today. I'll be right over here. Are you nervous?

TENOR: No.

MARIA: Good. What's your name?

TENOR: Tony.

MARIA: Tony? Just Tony?

TENOR: You mean when I sing! Anthony Candolino.

MARIA: I always mean when you sing. I only mean when you sing. This is a master class, not a psychiatrist's office. Are any of you out there undergoing psychiatry? I hope not. Tell us about yourself. Your training. Your professional experience, if any. Your hopes, your dreams.

TENOR: I have a BA in music from USC and an MFA in voice from UCLA.

MARIA: Go on.

TENOR: I've done Billy Jackrabbit in *Fanciulla del West* with Opera Ohio and I'm covering Rinuccio in *Gianni Schicchi* for Opera West.

MARIA: We all have to begin somewhere. You haven't told us about your dreams.

TENOR: I want to be a great singer. Like you. I want to be rich and famous. Like you. I want it all. Like you. Move over, Richard Tucker. Here comes Tony Candolino.

MARIA: May I have more water, please?

(*There is a longish pause.*)

TENOR: Are we waiting for your water?

MARIA: No, we're waiting for you.

TENOR: I've chosen *Tosca*.

(*The* STAGEHAND *enters with another pitcher of water.*)

Cavaradossi's aria, the first act.

MARIA: I can tell you right now: if you hold the B-flat longer than the composer asks for, it's going to be off with your extremely handsome head.

(To the STAGEHAND:) Thank you.

(To the TENOR:) No showing off, eh?

TENOR: I'll be happy if I get the B-flat, period.

MARIA: No happier than we.

STAGEHAND: You're welcome.

(*He exits.*)

(*The* ACCOMPANIST *begins to play the introduction to "Recondita armonia" from Puccini's* Tosca.)

MARIA: Just a moment, Tony. Feelings like Sharon's: we use them, we don't give them away on some voodoo witch doctor's couch. Again.

(*The* ACCOMPANIST *plays; the* TENOR *begins to sing.*)

TENOR: "Dammi i colori."

MARIA: I'm going to stop you.

TENOR: I got more out than the soprano did. You stopped her at "Oh."

MARIA: This is no joke. I don't know why you're smiling.

TENOR: I wasn't smiling.

MARIA: Was he smiling?

TENOR: I'm sorry.

Master Class

MARIA: You're either going to flirt with the public or we're going to work. Which is it going to be?

TENOR: Work.

MARIA: Now what were you doing?

TENOR: Nothing. I was singing.

MARIA: You were right the first time. You were *just* singing, which equals nothing. Again.

(*The* ACCOMPANIST *begins again.*)

TENOR: (singing) "Dammi i colori."

MARIA: Where are you?

TENOR: You mean right now? Or in the opera?

MARIA: No games, Tony.

TENOR: I'm in Rome, I'm in a church, I'm painting a picture. I just asked the old Sacristan for my paints. That's what "Dammi i colori" means: "Give me the paints."

MARIA: What church? Whose picture? Quick, quick. I don't have all day.

TENOR: I don't know. St. Patrick's! No, that's in. St. Peter's? St. Somebody's! Whose portrait? Some woman's obviously. Tosca's? No. The Mona Lisa, I don't know!

MARIA: So, let me get this straight. You don't know where you are, you are about to paint a portrait but you don't know of whom, and yet you are about to sing an aria. No wonder people don't like opera.

TENOR: I don't think you have to know all those things. I have a voice, I have a technique, I even have a B-flat.

MARIA: So do I. It's not enough.

TENOR: It was for Mario Lanza. I'm sorry, I love Mario Lanza. He's my hero. So kill me.

MARIA: You haven't done your homework, Tony.

TENOR: I just came out here to sing for you.

MARIA: I'm not interested in just singing.

TENOR: Sing and get your feedback.

MARIA: My what? My "feedback"? What an ugly word. What is feedback? He wants my feedback. I don't give feedback.

TENOR: Your response.

MARIA: I respond to what I feel. I feel nothing but anger for someone who so little treasures his art. You're not prepared, Mr. Tony Tight Pants. Go home. You're wasting our time. Next student.

TENOR: No.

MARIA: No?

TENOR: No.

MARIA: That's the first interesting thing you've said since you came out here.

TENOR: I came here to sing.

MARIA: You weren't ready.

TENOR: I'm going to sing.

MARIA: And I can't stop you?

TENOR: I need your help. I want to sing. I want to sing well. I know I have a voice and I know it's not enough. I want to be an artist.

>   (*He sings:*) "Dammi i colori."

>   (*To* MARIA:) Please.

(MARIA *nods to the* ACCOMPANIST, *who begins again.*)

MARIA: You're in the church of Sant' Andrea della Valle, just off the Corso. Do you know Rome?

TENOR: No.

MARIA: It doesn't matter. It's 10 A.M. on a beautiful spring morning. You made love all night to Floria Tosca, the most beautiful woman in Rome. And now you're painting another woman, unobserved, as she prays to the Blessed Mother. They're both beautiful, but it's Tosca's body against yours you feel. Now sing.

TENOR: It doesn't say anything about 10 A.M. or spring or Tosca's body in the score.

MARIA: It should say it in your imagination. Otherwise you have notes, nothing but notes.

Master Class

Sing!

TENOR: "Rencondita armonia."

MARIA: On the breath, on the breath!

TENOR: "di bellezze diverse!"

MARIA: Don't force.

TENOR: "È bruna Floria."

MARIA: Much better.

TENOR: "l'ardente amante mia."

MARIA: You're singing about your mistress! Look happy.

ACCOMPANIST: "Scherza coi fanti e lascia stare i santi!"

TENOR: *Bravo!*

MARIA: Concentrate.

TENOR:

> "E te, beltade ignota,
> cinta di chiome bionde,
> tu azzurro hai l'occhio,
> Tosca ha l'occhio nero"

MARIA: (*at will, during the above*) That's right, open it up. Let me feel that blond hair. Blue eyes. Tosca's black eyes now.

ACCOMPANIST: "Scherza coi fanti e lascia stare i santi!"

MARIA: (*as before*) Do you know what you're singing about, Tony?

(*He shakes his head while continuing to sing.*)

Art, in all its mystery, blends these different beauties together. One woman, one ideal!

TENOR:

> "L'arte nel suo mistero
> le diverse bellezze insiem confonde:"

MARIA: Here it comes. The Big Tune! Go for it!

TENOR:

> "ma, nel ritrar costei . . .
>
> il mio solo pensiero,
>
> ah! il mio sol pensier sei tu,
>
> Tosca, sei tu!"

(MARIA *silently mouths the final high notes along with the* TENOR.)

(*The music ends.* MARIA *is silent.*)

MARIA: That was beautiful. I have nothing more to say. That was beautiful.

TENOR: I've also prepared *Werther* and "Ah, sì, ben mio."

MARIA: That won't be necessary. Are we scheduled for a break now? No? Great music always takes so much out of me. I feel quite faint. That will be all, Mr. Candoloro.

TENOR: You can call me Tony.

MARIA: I wish you well on your career.

TENOR: Thank you. Don't you have any advice for me?

MARIA: Remember the springtime. Now go.

(*He goes.* MARIA *sits in the chair.*)

The
Callas Cult

(an excerpt from The Queen's Throat*)*

Wayne Koestenbaum

*Yale professor Koestenbaum is passionate
about Callas. In this striking and original
portrait, he struggles to understand why—
and in the process gives her back her
humanity.*

Maria Callas, immortal, died on September 16, 1977. I've seen documentary footage of mourners sobbing outside her funeral: as the hearse drives away, disconsolate fans applaud the departing body and cheer "Brava Callas!"—grimly acknowledging that she will give no more performances, that she will never hear this applause, that she craved applause and died for lack of it. To mourn Maria Callas: there, cult happiness begins.

She was Callas long before she died, but she would be a little less Callas if she were still living. Untimely death assists her legend and connects her to themes that have shadowed gay culture: premature mortality, evanescence, solitude.

I never heard Callas perform in person. I am a post-Callas opera queen, looking back. I confess that during her life I knew of her only in the role of Aristotle Onassis's mistress. Even now, I don't have an exemplary collection of Callas recordings or a thorough command of Callas lore.

Listening to Callas posthumously, I feel like a necrophiliac: but haven't other gays fallen guiltily in love with departed matter? To be a dandy—a useless thing!—is to waste time and fortune; and the worshipper of Callas *is* a waste, going nowhere with his feelings.

Callas became an international star in the early 1950s, a time when gay people, though silent and secret, and seeking assimilation and acceptance rather than radical action, were developing a rich culture. Callas remains the operatic diva most closely (if only tacitly) associated with gay fandom. . . .

Here are a dozen attempts to explain the gay cult of Callas. But it's impossible to circumscribe love. As a commentator, one can only operate like a skylight at a premiere, advertising a location.

I

Ask a gay man, a Callas nut, why he loves Callas, and he may say, "Because she's the best." We need to like the best. (Excuse the "we." I say "we" without knowing the group's contours. "We" are not all alike. I say "we" wishfully, hypothetically.) We have been considered the dregs, and so we have constructed hierarchies of taste in which—sometimes against reason—we elevate certain stars to the summit. Because she recorded the soprano repertoire so exhaustively, because every historian and journalist knows she was her era's operatic divinity, and because everyone agrees she transformed the repertoire by reviving forgotten coherences of song and drama—for these reasons we're doing nothing exceptional by loving Callas. We pretend we like her for solely musical reasons. She's a safe object of adoration. She has snob appeal. She recorded for Angel. What opera lover doesn't recognize and revere Callas, despite querulous, catty reservations? And yet because of the flaws in her voice, the taste for Callas allows room for argument. To prove Callas' worth, a posthumous, dispersed claque emerges—a nation of solitudes.

It is marvelous to adore a queen so undisputed, so deserving; to contribute to a cultural phenomenon (the Callas revolution) that isn't a back room or a closet.

Luchino Visconti, in a photograph, kisses Callas's cheek, which makeup foundation has made unnaturally pale; Leonard Bernstein exclaims, "Callas? She was pure electricity." Visconti and Bernstein loved Callas not because they were gay but because she was a genius;

The Callas Cult

it is easy and conventional to deny the link between a woman's artistry and a gay man's sympathetic rapture. Bernstein and Visconti would probably have rejected my reductive association of Callas fandom and gay identity. They loved Callas simply because she was sublime. But sublimity has particular currency in gay culture.

Greatness of Callas's sort requires reiteration. The comet is gone in a moment; someone needs to stand around afterward and praise it, recall it, verify it. Callas still needs promulgators. Even now, she seems to demand a jury—of gay men—to vote her Not Guilty.

2

I worship her because she made mistakes, and because she seemed to value expressivity over loveliness. We don't believe in nature anymore, but Callas put forth the effect of nature as opposed to the appearance of order, and offered an acceptable, digestible anarchy, a set of sounds on the verge of chaos—but enjoyably so. Here lay the danger, the lure: she was a mess *and* she was a goddess.

Her voice gave evidence of long attempts to domesticate the unacceptable. Recording producer Walter Legge commented that in her muted middle range she sounded as if she were singing into a bottle. (Sometimes in her middle range I feel I am traveling on a tour of her sinuses.) Enjoying Callas's muffled voice, one declared affinity with hidden things.

Her voice dramatically took advantage of the listener's assumption that the opera would go as planned. She ambushed. In Mexico City in 1950 she unfurled a high E-flat without warning, dominating tenor and chorus at the end of the Triumphal Scene in *Aida*. Though her mediocre costar, tenor Kurt Baum, was furious, the audience loved her unexpected domination. Classical music may seem to demand servility of its performers, but with her high E-flat, Callas stopped serving.

Callas's upper register wobbled—a "flap." With time, the flap grew less controlled. Commenting on a 1955 *Aida*, John Ardoin points out her "flapping high C through which the Egyptian army could have marched." Too much wobbling may sound indecent, schizoid, but to Callas's fans, the indecency was endurable and gratifying. Lapses made her a sympathetic figure, a vocal underdog. Some notes, pressed too hard, turned to steel; and when we heard the steel we sympathized with her plight. The steel and the wobble announced a predicament; we loved the mistakes because they seemed autobiographical, because without mediation or guile they wrote a naked heart's wound. And if her notes had a tendency to wobble, to grow harsh, then this possibility of failure gave her fans a function. The infallible performance does not require an audience.

Callas's unattractive sounds forced her audience to reevaluate the difference between the beautiful and the grotesque, and spoke to gays, who have often made use, as spectators and creators, of the gothic. From homophobic culture's point of view, a gay person's soul is a haunted house full of moldering antechambers and dead-end staircases. Can a gay interior be lovely? Or is it, at best, plush?

With peerless technique (I'd call it a form of insouciance if it weren't so intensely willed) she hid her flaws, and curbed her unconventional, through-a-glass-darkly timbre. In her Paris 1961 rendition of Thomas's "Je suis Titania," she holds an awkward high note for its full value, even though the tone is unpleasant; she outstares the ugliness, dares it to ruin her good time. In her 1957 *Manon Lescaut* or in her 1964 *Tosca*, she prepares for the ambiguous high notes with such control of phrase and rhythm and portamento and pitch and attack, that we acquiesce, and forgive, and imagine that the note's wretched aspects are a mirror, reflecting the greedy demands *we* make of the singer, and asking us: "How would *you* manage such a note?"

During the harsh high note, we are closer to Callas. We befriend her. Through error, she seems to implore: "Art is punishment, and I am vulnerable. Have you ever been exposed, opened up in public? Find parallels in your life to this almost unacceptable note that will make the audience hiss."

The Callas Cult

3

We love Callas because she revised her body. In three years she dropped from 210 pounds to 144, and changed from ugly duckling to glamour queen. Bodies can't always be altered, but Callas's self-revision, like a sex change, makes us believe in the power of wish.

Careers with gay followings often have moments of rupture and reinvention: moments when the star's body or persona radically shifts, and proves the former self to have been a fabrication. The gay fan, schooled in the gap between public manner and private feeling, may identify less with Callas's newfound glamour than with her former plainness; or he may identify with the rift between the two. Callas revised her image twice: when she lost weight, and when she lost her voice. Her body was a liability she had the power to revise; her voice was a virtue she lacked the power to retain. (Even when Callas had a voice, she seemed to be losing it: and so a gay interpretation of Callas's career was always, from the start, possible.)

We know and adore the difference between the queen's two bodies: plump awkward Callas in Athens before her fame; slimmed Callas with dyed blonde hair, for the Visconti production of *Vestale*; Callas in Egyptian drag—dressed as Queen Hatshepsut—at the 1957 Waldorf Astoria Imperial Ball. Callas in fancy dress was one of the marvels of the 1950s, for, like her idol Audrey Hepburn, she embodied a Wildean stylization of manner and gesture, as if the depths were dull and lethal and it were salutary to hover on the surface. The typical Hepburn plot traced her transit from pixie quirkiness to obvious beauty: in *Sabrina*, *Funny Face*, or *My Fair Lady*, no one knows that Hepburn is a knockout until a couturier gets hold of her. But while Hepburn seemed born to be beautiful, Callas had an effortful, wounded relationship to her glamour. What she couldn't wear when she was fat, she wore with spite when she was thin. And she did not make neat distinctions between art and costume. "I want my art to be the most perfect," she wrote to her husband. "I also want what I wear to be the nicest that exists." At her loveliest, she looks vindictive: she will make people pay for their former indifference.

Her operatic performances seemed real; her real life seemed operatic. Since Oscar Wilde, this confusion between mask and truth has been a cornerstone of gay culture. Even in private life (if we call "private" the studied scenes of Callas at the airport, at Maxim's, at dressmaker Madame Biki's), she painted her eyes in the Medea style: long kohl lines, like a latter-day Cleopatra. The excessive eyeliner proved that she was in charge of her image, that her face was a tablet on which she wrote her life, and that femininity was a lot of work. The labor's reward? Saying "I told you so" to a cruel world. Callas's radical weight loss, and her stylized approach to matters of dress and makeup, gave poignance to her life's plot: she seemed, despite her fame and wealth, a victim of the gender system.

Callas's "Audrey Hepburn" persona—the perfectly groomed society lady—was particularly camp when seen against her feud with her mother, Evangelia Callas, who wrote a scandalous exposé entitled *My Daughter Maria Callas*. (Evangelia's own excesses are exposed in *Sisters*, the confessions of Jackie Callas, Maria's sister.) Mrs. Callas publicized her work as jewelry saleswoman at the shop of Jolie Gabor (mother of Zsa Zsa and Eva) to humiliate Maria for refusing to send money. Maria wrote to her mother: "Don't come to us with your troubles. I had to work for my money, and you are young enough to work, too. If you can't make enough money to live on, you can jump out of the window or drown yourself." No ordinary gal, Callas had the effrontery to break with her mother *and* dress up.

Queen Callas emerged from the chrysalis of the dumpy diva; another fabled trajectory was rootless, nationless Maria turning into a Greek woman profoundly identified with her homeland. Her apotheosis was singing Norma at Epidaurus; some say her voice had a quintessentially Greek timbre. As a Greek, Callas was an outsider to La Scala, Covent Garden, the Paris Opéra, the Met—turfs she conquered: the outsider who enters a field and vanquishes all opposition is an appealing figure, and not only to gays. Born Maria Anna Cecilia Sophia Kalogeropoulos, Maria Callas was imagined to hide an authentic and exotic Greek nature, which explained her notorious romance with Aristotle Onassis, and which gave her the status of a goddess, just as her overweight and impoverished beginnings emphasized a "realness"—a stigma, a wound—beneath the jet-set splendor.

The Callas Cult

4

We love Callas because she disciplined her voice. The realm of discipline is itself a part of gay culture: weight lifters, S/M—pageants of control and self-mastery. Callas cleaned up her voice with excruciating and exhilarating thoroughness, and disciplined her phrases as severely as she disciplined her servants. She gave her staff an authoritarian list of house rules: "When you are summoned by us, you will come immediately, and always perfectly dressed"; "One will never say no to what has been asked, and no more of that 'Yes, sir' 'Yes, ma'am' nonsense"; "Everyone, including the housekeeper, will wash and iron their own garments, especially intimate items." At home and on stage, Callas commanded.

Callas was a trouper, a perfectionist: on time to rehearsals, willing to sing an aria again and again to get it right. Musical exactitude justified her caprices, and proved to her detractors that she behaved strictly, without excess or indulgence. She spoke fondly of doing vocal exercises, and of various mentors. Of Tullio Serafin, she said, "I'm afraid he's the last of those kind of maestri." She loves the word "maestri" and the notion of mastery. When Callas gives every damned pitch in a difficult run from *Lucia* or *Norma* (another singer would not be so thorough and clean), or when she reminds my listening ear that there is a vast difference between eighth notes and triplets, or between half steps and whole steps, her precision makes my mouth gape, and tells me how callused her feet must be from walking without shoes this far up the hill to magnificence.

Maria Callas, like Joan Crawford's Mildred Pierce, was a model of the career woman who succeeds only because she is viciously ambitious and because she has given up her capacities to be a good daughter and a good mother. One can enjoy the self-lashing aspects of Callas's career, however, and jettison the underlying antifeminist moral, by taking Maria Callas as proof that roles can be reversed, that destinies can be chosen (whether or not it is actually possible to alter the material conditions underlying our fates). The story of Callas, a fable, makes us believe in the power of individual fantasy. Similarly, we imagine that *choosing to be gay*, even at the cost of martyrdom, is a cataclysmic act, capable of transforming private destinies and public systems.

Callas swore by these axioms: *Study the words of an opera, and you will understand how to color the note or shape the phrase. Give each note its proper value and weight, and you will reveal the score's internal mysteries.* Each musical moment stamped with Callas-the-perfectionist simultaneously thrills us by its sublimity ("Thank God I am alive to hear this phrase from the *Barbiere* sung so accurately") and by its masochism ("She sacrificed so much to achieve this perfection, and may I, by God's grace, learn to find ennobling uses for my inborn or acquired masochisms").

We love her for intruding, via magisterial discipline, such a range of mannerisms—a control of how a phrase might always, every moment, *mean* something. This control made her an avatar of speakability, of the ability to say painful and illuminating truths and to shroud those truths in a medium that leaves its messages shadowy and subliminal. Music conceals the arguments it sinuously advances. We consider music to be merely expressive. But when "expressivity" happens, something particular is usually being expressed.

Sometimes her singing sounds like weeping. The suffering seems to arise from the discipline of music-making, and the discipline of woman-making.

5

She's irretrievable and so I want to retrieve her. She departed before the world could surround her with sufficient adulation. Evanescence and transience: modern gay literatures are obsessed with the desire to be immortal and to press against the moment's confines. Gay figurehead Blanche DuBois mooned, "Don't you just love these long rainy afternoons in New Orleans when an hour isn't just an hour—but a little piece of eternity dropped into your hands . . . ?"

Callas sang in the era of *Sunset Boulevard*: in legend, she became a Norma Desmond, unable to bear very much reality, dreaming of impossible comebacks. After the affair with

Onassis began, she had a vocal crisis, retired, and then returned to the stage. She collapsed at the Paris Opéra after the third act of *Norma*; she sang one more *Tosca* in London, and then she never sang an opera again. She returned to the recording studio; the results were too ambiguous for release. She taught master classes in 1971 and 1972 at Juilliard. I love the picture of Callas at Juilliard in black pants-suit and dour reading glasses because I love to see a divinity become practical and serve a function: I love to see majesty drop to earth in no-nonsense black, majesty in need of glasses, majesty in the fashions of 1971, which were flattering to no one. She returned to the stage with di Stefano in 1973–74 for a world tour of duo recitals: a voice in ruins, say witnesses. The has-been inhabits a mythical neighborhood. I am not a has-been. I am, like most fans, a never-been. Has-beens and never-beens have much in common. And so I visited the Avenue Georges Mandel, in Paris, where Callas lived, isolated, before her death; I wanted to experience that neighborhood of silence. I wanted to verify the photograph I've stared at so long: an often reprinted shot of Callas opening or shutting the curtains of a spacious window that looks like it never lets in light, an image of a soul shut into a role and not knowing the way out. Zeffirelli's movie of *La Traviata*, an elegy, an homage to Callas, a memorial to her vanished voice, shows us Violetta's apartment, first, from the outside. We see Violetta's window; it is just like Callas's! That aloof window is the sign of a grandeur and a sickness—a consumption—forever closed. Think of the spaces shut to us. Think of the rooms—our rooms—we have never named. Voice is a room: it opens, for an instant, in a great operatic career. But most of the time the room is closed off to knowledge and to memory.

On the cover of Callas's reissued recordings are photographs of the singer after retirement, to underscore the tragedy of the woman who outlived her voice. She smiles, radiant in simple outfits and pearl earrings—but we know better. We know she is miserable. We know the record within the sleeve contains the trace of her past; Callas and her legendary voice have parted company. Gay people have compensated for silence by enjoying the ironic or tragic transformation of power into pathos. We relish falls. Sublimity turns into degradation, and our interest quickens—not because we are sadistic sickos but because we like to see reputations, or the very idea of "reputation," decompose.

6

When we value Callas for creating a revolution in operatic performance practice, for singing neglected Bellini and Donizetti operas as if they were tragic vehicles of undiminished power, we are valuing her for opening up the opera box, the closed space of a genre that never seemed to let us in or to let our meanings out. And yet, ironically, her revitalizations of dismissed *bel canto* operas only emphasized opera's moribund nature.

Innovators like Peter Sellars highlight opera's anachronism, and turn opera's liability into an expressive strength. Anachronism was one aspect of opera that long ago opened it to gay appropriation; opera seemed campy and therefore available to gay audiences only when it had become an outdated art form, sung in foreign languages, with confused, implausible plots. Opera's apparent distance from contemporary life made it a refuge for gays, who were creations of modern sexual systems, and yet whom society could not acknowledge or accommodate. Opera is not very real. But gayness has never been admitted into the precincts of reality. And so gays may seek out art that does not respect the genuine.

Superficially, Maria Callas took away opera's campiness by making it believable and vivid. And yet by importing truth into opera, an art of the false, she gave the gay fan a dissonance to match his own. Bestowing verisimilitude on Lucia or Norma or Elvira, Callas perforated the operagoer's complacency; her voice and her presence, arsenals of *depth*, when brought to bear on music that had become *superficial*, upset the audience's sense of perspective. Though it seems sacrilegious to call Callas's musically compelling creations *camp*, she performed the same kind of reversal that camp induces: she shattered the codes that separate dead from living works of art. To crosscut rapidly between yesterday and today is an effect that, in different circumstances, we recognize as camp. Callas "camped" *Lucia* not by mocking it (Lucia is too easy to mock) but by taking it seriously. Resuscitating *Lucia*, Callas challenged our belief that history's movement is linear, that there is a difference between past and present, and that modern reality is real.

7

We love her because she incarnated vocal multiplicity and heterogeneity. She had three voices: chest tones like a contralto, an inconsistent, cloudy, yet beautiful middle register, and a piercing top that was fleet in coloratura but often metallic. One colleague said that Callas had three hundred voices. Callas, a chameleon, stepped in and out of registers like quick costume changes.

But she was often criticized for multiplicity. She couldn't cross over the bridge between voices and then make the bridge vanish. We often heard the bridge; and so her voice seemed a Cubist painting composed of angles not organized into easily interpretable wholes—an eye, a nose, a brow.

Like *The Three Faces of Eve*, Callas's vocal split-personality affliction was a timely image of what society believed to be woman's intrinsically various and Circean nature. And gay men could identify with this vision of fractured woman: Callas's divided voice seemed to mirror the queer soul's incoherences.

Callas became famous for singing *Die Walküre* and *I Puritani* three days apart at Teatro La Fenice, and for taking only a week to learn *Puritani*. In one throat, she reconciled two vocal types—the dramatic soprano and the coloratura lyric. Even her rival Renata Tebaldi admitted the pleasurable shock of hearing Callas's heavy voice in the light repertoire. Callas's assumption of *bel canto* roles, after establishing credentials as a dramatic soprano, was an affront to fixed vocal categories and to the gendered distinctions built into them. Commentators describe Callas as a reincarnation of a kind of singer that flourished in opera's golden age—a singer who could span all ranges and styles. We admire Callas for exceeding and giving the lie to modern measurements. No note she sings remains the same; she changes voice *inside* the note, as if to say: "Try to catch me, to name me, to confine me in your brutalizing classifications!"

Every body is a civil war. Callas sang the war.

Most singers of Callas's caliber hide the register break. Callas couldn't. The naked break shows her to be, though a genius, a bit of a freak—delightfully self-embarrassing, unable to control herself in this tiny matter on which *bel canto* art depends. The break between registers is the moment when the voice proves itself to be of two minds. Compare her 1953 *Lucia* and her 1959 *Lucia*: although her tone is darker in the 1959 version, her register break is tranquilized, and so she travels up and down without disgrace—a subdued Callas, a Callas about to quit.

Callas took in breath dramatically, audibly, as if she were gasping. She turned the need to breathe into an expressive opportunity. But the gasp also revealed the cost of music-making: phrases need to come from somewhere in the body—some lode, undiscovered, where power sleeps. The gasp is the price tag on the expensive garment of the aria.

Words like "gay" or "queer" are crude, and Callas would not have approved of them. But I imagine she would have approved of this task: revealing the abjection and the sadness that lie buried in listening.

8

I adore Callas because she so frequently expresses fury—a wrath that is its own reward and its own argument, that seeks no external justification, that makes no claim beyond the pleasure of drive, of emotion, of expressing *why I have been wronged*. A tribunal, she doesn't just express what *she* feels, but expresses what the *universe* should feel about her predicament. Every great Callas phrase of jealousy and fury becomes a command: "Universe, listen! Universe, obey! Universe, assume my point of view!" And we have visual images for her voice's tendency to radiate anger: think of Callas as Medea or Tosca, holding the knife, her eyes shooting sparks, her painted mouth a line-drawing of rage—as in the "tigress" photo taken backstage in Chicago when process servers tried to hand her a summons.

But sometimes she sings like an innocent. John Ardoin calls this sound her "little girl" voice. She mutes the tone, makes it reedy and demure, holds back power. She uses this restrained voice to impersonate virgins like Amina, or to mark the difference, in a role like Butterfly or Lucia, between schoolgirl piety and murderous maturity. Pretending to be innocent, she portrays, instead, her detachment from naïve states. This coy voice sets in relief the rage she more frequently and convincingly expresses. (Sometimes the "little girl' voice doesn't convey innocence, but a spectral emptiness.)

Gay men may identify with demonstrations of female wrath and willfulness because such behavior so wholeheartedly exceeds the bounds of acceptable gender behavior; displays of masculine power are alienating and depressing (they reflect patriarchy's sway), but displays of feminine power show the universe executing an about-face. Her vengeful volleys give us courage, and inspire us as we struggle to be open and not closed, serene and not erased, human and not degenerate.

I feast on her walkouts, her cancellations, or the scandals emanating from these outbursts, which have nothing to do with music, but which seem to emerge from her vocalism, her sudden flashes of chest tone, her searing, firecracker diction—the rolled "r" and the pugnacious dental and the narrow, nasal, oblong vowel: these terrifying effects denote revenge, murder, and the realm of wish, pushed to pathetic yet enviable extremes.

She fought impresarios and conductors—a feud with Serafin because he recorded *Traviata* with another soprano, Antonietta Stella; battles with Rudolf Bing; the Edinburgh cancellation; the time she threatened to brain a hostile impresario with a bronze inkstand and then— her husband said she weighed over two hundred pounds—forcefully drew her knee into the offender's stomach. But the most famous disobedience was the Rome walkout. Although ill, Callas was persuaded to sing a scheduled gala performance of *Norma*; the Rome Opera had hired no cover, and Italy's president was in the audience. Callas sang the first act, but was in poor voice. When she refused to go on for the second act, management begged her at least to speak her lines. Adamant, she left the theater through an underpass, like the Phantom of the Opera: "Scandale!"

One can purchase a pirate recording of that failed first act (I've withstood the temptation): I imagine that the record circulates primarily among gay fans who love, as I do, the aura of a woman who walks out of the closet of her role, defies the president, and places her throat's health over an opera house's rules.

About the furor, Callas later said, with her inimitable, blinkered rhetoric of self-defense: "There was a lawsuit. We fought twice, and I won twice. I had deceived nobody. I never do. I am a very simple woman, and I am a very moral woman. I do not mean that I claim to be a 'good' woman, as the word is: that is for others to judge; but I am a moral woman in that I see clearly what is right and wrong for me, and I do not confuse them or evade them."

Adoring Callas, I am admiring breakdown, resistance, walkout, flight, and feud.

9

Because of the Tebaldi-Callas feud, choosing isn't a neutral or pacific experience. It means taking sides, and shutting down the faculties of sympathy and softness.

Callas called Tebaldi her "dear colleague and friend," but Renata, unable to match the breadth of Maria's repertoire, finally left "the Scala." "Rivals I have not," claimed Callas. Eventually the two women embraced backstage after a 1968 Tebaldi opening-night Met performance of *Adriana Lecouvreur* (Maria had already retired).

Even on records, Callas seems to require devotion, not toleration; to enjoy Callas, one must renounce Tebaldi's virtues, and adopt Callas as a cause-for-life. Though Callas often piously thanked God for her good fortune, as if God cared about Callas's career, her fan must forswear decency and embrace the pleasure of partisanship; the Callas claque is an

The Callas Cult

underworld order, like a revolutionary cadre, the Communist party, or the Mattachine Society.

Fetishist that I am, I focus my shame on the word "Callas." I'm embarrassed to say the name as she and her crowd said it—the huge A, CAH-LAAAS, neither syllable emphasized at the cost of the other, the two syllables distinct from any others in the world. Saying "Callas" fills my mouth with fruity sensation. "Callas," an odd, invented name, is a telling near-anagram of Pablo *Casals*, cellist who nobly refused to play in Spain after Franco came to power, and who performed at the Kennedy White House. Casals represented the interpreter as a saint; Callas, too, was a kind of saint, but a rearranged one. Turn the word "Callas" inside out: fans at La Scala cheering "sCalla sCalla sCalla sCalla," as if Callas were the container as well as the object contained.

Deciding to love Callas, you fall into a category; the Callas fan. It's a sweet, drowsy membership: I can stare all day at the photograph of Callas in offstage life wearing a veil and white gloves and pearls, her ineffably sad eyes elongated by makeup, her ears large, her mien arrogant and refined, her regal brutishness distinct from her musicianship, which was a matter of gift, work, intelligence. . . . Built into the love of Callas is a fear of not doing her justice, never doing her justice; the attempt to account for the love of Callas is a sham and a transgression.

10

All divas, when they sing, when they emerge from apprenticeship into the spotlight, come out: but Callas came out vocally, with unique flamboyance, at a time when coming out was nearly impossible for queers. Even within operatic singing's straitjacket (Callas used the word "straitjacketing" to describe the first stage of studying a new role—that phase when she learned the notes exactly as they were written), she appeared always to be exposing a secret shame and a corresponding power. She was celebrated for tailoring phrases in an opera to suit a specific extramusical situation—for aiming a death-threat line at the box of La Scala's impresario, Antonio Ghiringhelli, or giving a rendition of Medea in Dallas with a fury that seemed directed at Rudolf Bing, who had just canceled her Met contract.

Her uniquely emotive singing style parallels the Method acting that was fashionable in 1950s North American cinema (Brando, Dean, Clift, Monroe). Method acting is a style of the closet and of the closet's collapse: the actor brings private, undisclosable woes to bear on the part. And yet the strain and effort in Method performances—the seething and stammering and stumbling—prove the sturdiness of the walls locking in the not-yet-spoken self. The performer needs to grunt and moan and cry in order to break through the policed border between private and public. Callas makes us sick of camouflage. After hearing Callas, who could tolerate the closet? And yet the evidence of Callas's broken spirit makes us nostalgic for the closet. Maybe, for a moment, we want to step back in.

II

It is easy to see why Callas appeals to the drag queen in me, because Callas in motion (I rely on the evidence of films) is a sinuous, studied spectacle that one could forever simulate but never match: long arms, hands gliding slowly toward the shoulders to acknowledge thunderous applause, large nose and archaic eyes, hair usually piled in a voluminous chignon but sometimes loose and sometimes flat as Hepburn's Left Bank bob in *Funny Face*, each different hairdo transforming Callas's features so it's hard to know precisely what she looks like. I don't want to steal, imitate, or distort Callas's gestures. But I notice them, and I feel noticed *by* them; her greedy manipulation of physical space draws me into fuller life, even if, on the day of her funeral, September 20, 1977, I was marking my nineteenth birthday, and had never heard of Maria Callas, whose voice and image would posthumously drape tapestries over me.

Her speaking voice was odd; she always seemed to be setting the record straight, or proving herself to be oblique as a Modigliani, simulating behaviors she couldn't pass off as genuine. Her English was affected, and full of non sequiturs. In an interview, she said: "Every time a taxi driver recognizes me it astonishes me. It irritates me. You know, I don't go out very much. I don't put myself on exhibit. I live in seclusion. I am wild. Very."

Only the banality of an exceptional person, like Callas, has the power to induce in the observer that dizzy pleasurable sensation of identification which is my subject here. Rilke wanted the angels to answer him. He knew they wouldn't. Every modern sad soul wants an answer from the void; Callas is one figure to whom some gay men have recently looked for reciprocation and confirmation. Confirmation of what? Life's grimness, and the power of expressivity to alleviate the grimness, or to give the illusion of succor.

Late in her short life, she begged Tito Gobbi to take her out for an ice cream. She imagined that the world had abandoned her. The epigraph to Charles Ludlam's *Galas*: "Only my dogs will not betray me."

12

In a photograph, Visconti wraps his arms tightly around Callas and kisses her on the cheek—it looks to be a firm, authentic kiss—and she smiles, flattered and gratified to be kissed; Zeffirelli, doughy and devoted, kisses Callas, and she smiles radiantly, knowing the limits of the kiss; Bernstein holds Callas's hands and studies her, and they seem to be playing a seesaw game, figuring out whether their bodies are equivalent; gaunt and shirtless, Pasolini directs Callas as Medea, and she is attentive, obediently holding her hands to her face. These photographs attest to a specific historic configuration: the gay man venerating the theatrical woman and the woman responding gaily, the woman imitating the gay man and the gay man imitating the woman, the gay man directing and then listening and admiring, the man and woman collaborating.

Poring over Callas, I'm like Manuel Puig's Molina, the gay window-dresser in *Kiss of the Spider Woman*, who sustains his cellmate and himself in prison by reciting the plots of movies.

One of the movies he recites is Nazi propaganda. But Molina doesn't understand the film's sinister ideology. He thinks it is a wonderful romance. His love for stars blinds him to political emergencies.

Of course I feel guilty for my imaginary romance with Callas's voice. But I don't know who is harmed by the worship. Certainly not Callas. Are you harmed? I imagine that you harbor similar attachments, that you, too, send your love to a vague, aloof star in the cultural firmament, a radiance that will never reward you with a glance, though you have spent your life in patient, earnest, fruitless attendance.

Visconti said of Callas that she was "a monstrous phenomenon. Almost a sickness—the kind of actress that has passed for all time." Is Callas, within gay culture, the embodiment of "homosexuality" as the monstrosity we are and abhor and adore? No, Callas was not a sickness. Callas was a refuge, where a forbidden sexuality, a forbidden alienation from masculinity, could spread its wings. Listening to Callas, I acquire spaciousness. If consciousness, as determined by gender and sexuality, has certain limits, a voice like Callas's has the power to turn the mind's closed room into an immensity: she bestows the illusion that the view continues endlessly on the other side of the mirror, and that wherever you expected to confront limits, instead you find continuations.

I have been speaking about gayness as if I knew what it meant. I don't. It is a mirage.

Gayness isn't my rock-bottom nature. Rather, I listen *for* and *toward* gayness: I approach it as one approaches a vanishing point, or as one tries to match a pitch that is fading into a vast silence.

Walter Legge, who produced many of Callas's legendary recordings, once peered inside her mouth and remarked that it was shaped like a Gothic cathedral. In imagination I am staring into Callas's mouth to see her upper palate's high spires—like far Christminster to Thomas Hardy's Jude, who gazes at the horizon but will never reach the imaginary city that gleams there.

The Callas Cult

Death by Enthusiasm

Hector Berlioz

(translated by Jacques Barzun)

*During his lifetime, Hector Berlioz was bet-
ter known for bravura orchestrations and
newspaper criticism than operas like* Les
Troyens. *Doubtless his own difficulties in the
cutthroat Paris music world colored this
acidly humorous portrait of a violinist who
would rather die than suffer bad art.*

I shall call my story *Death by Enthusiasm*. In 1808 a young musician had for three years been serving, with obvious distaste, as first violin in a theater in southern France. The boredom he carried with him every evening to the orchestra, where he had to play *The Barrel-Maker*, *The King and the Farmer*, *The Betrothed* or some such score of the kind, meant that he was looked upon by his colleagues as a stuck-up prig. "He thinks," said they, "that he alone in all the world has learning and taste; he scorns the opinion of the public, whose applause makes him shrug his shoulders, and also the opinion of other musicians, whom he affects to consider mere babes." His contemptuous laugh and impatient gestures every time that he had to play some platitude had repeatedly brought down on him severe reprimands from the conductor, and he would long ago have sent in his resignation if poverty, which always seems to choose for its victims temperaments of this sort, had not hopelessly hailed him to his post in front of a greasy and grimy old music-stand.

Adolphe D. obviously was one of those artists predestined to suffering; men who carry within themselves an ideal of the beautiful, pursue it unremittingly, and feel intense hatred for everything alien to it. Gluck, whose scores he knew by heart (for he had copied them in order to be better acquainted with them), was his idol. He read him, played him, and sang him night and day. A misguided amateur to whom he was giving lessons in solfeggio was once incautious enough to tell him that Gluck's operas were merely shouting and plainsong. D. flushed with indignation, yanked open the drawer of the desk, took from it the ten vouchers for the fees due him by this particular pupil, and flung them in his face, roaring: "Get out of here! I don't want you or your money, and if you ever step inside this door again, I will throw you out of the window!"

It is easy to see that with so much tolerance for his pupil's tastes, D. hardly made a fortune giving lessons. Spontini was just then in all his glory. The dazzling success of *La Vestale*, proclaimed by the thousand tongues of the press, made all the provincial dilettanti anxious to hear a score so touted by the Parisians. Accordingly the unfortunate theater managers strained themselves to circumvent, if not to overcome, the difficulties of staging and performing the new work.

Not wanting to lag behind, D.'s manager, like the rest, shortly annouced that *La Vestale* was in preparation. D., as is true of all fiery spirits whom a sound education has not taught to reason out their judgments, was an exclusivist in taste. He was at the outset full of prejudice against Spontini's opera, of which he knew not a single note: "They say it is in a new style, more melodic that Gluck's. So much the worse for the new style! Gluck's melody is good enough for me; the better is the enemy of the good. I bet it is detestable."

It was in this frame of mind that he took his seat in the orchestra on the day of the first stage rehearsal. As concertmaster he had not had to attend the earlier partial rehearsals. The other players, though they admired Lemoyne, found merit just the same in Spontini's score, and on seeing D. said among themselves: "Let's see what the great Adolphe's verdict about it is!" The latter went through the rehearsal without a word or a sign of either praise or blame. His ideas were undergoing a curious transformation. He realized fully from the very first scene that this was a noble and powerful work and that Spontini was a genius whose greatness he could not ignore. But not conceiving clearly what the composer's methods were, for they were new to

❧ 59 ❧   Death by Enthusiasm

him and the poor provincial performance made them still more difficult to grasp, D. borrowed the score, began by reading the words attentively, studied the spirit and character of the persons in the drama, then gave his whole mind to the analysis of the music, thus following a path that could not but lead him to a real and complete understanding of the opera as a perfect whole.

From that time forward it was noticed that he was becoming more and more sulky and taciturn; he evaded any questions put to him, or laughed sardonically when he heard his colleagues vent their admiration of Spontini. "Fools," he seemed to be saying, "how can you understand his work when you admire *The Betrothed?*"

Noticing the ironic expression on D.'s features, the players were sure that he judged Spontini as severely as he had Lemoyne, and that he bracketed both composers in one and the same reprobation. But one day when the performance was a trifle less execrable than usual, it was seen that the finale of the second act had moved him to tears, and they no longer knew what to think. "He is mad," said some; "he is play-acting," said others. And all together: "He is a second-rate musician."

Motionless in his chair, sunk in deep abstraction, and furtively wiping his eyes, D. said not a word to all this impertinence, but was hoarding a treasure of contempt and fury in his heart. The inadequacy of the orchestra, the even greater incompetence of the chorus, the lack of intelligence and feeling in the actors, the vocal ornaments added by the prima donna, the mutilation of every phrase and rhythm, the arrogant cuts—in short, the relentless beating and torturing he saw inflicted on the score which had become the object of his deepest worship and of which he knew every detail, caused him torments with which I am well-acquainted, but which I am unable to describe.

One night after the second act, the whole house having risen to its feet with cries of enthusiasm, D. felt fury overwhelm him; and an enraptured habitué asked him the commonplace question: "Well, M. Adolphe, what do you say?"

"I say," shouted D., pale with anger, "that you and all the others who are carrying on like lunatics in this theater are fools, asses, louts fit only to hear Lemoyne's music. If you weren't, you would break in the skulls of the manager, the singers, and the musicians, instead of condoning by your applause the most shameful profanation that genius can endure."

This time the insult was too great, and despite the fiery artist's performing talent, which made him invaluable; despite, also, the dreadful poverty which dismissal would entail, the manager could not avoid placating the public for the insult by relieving him of his duties.

Unlike the generality of men of his caliber, D. was not given to expensive tastes. He had some savings from his salary and from the lessons he had been giving, and was secure for three months at least. This cushioned the blow of his dismissal and even made him look upon it as likely to be useful for his artistic career by restoring his freedom. But the chief appeal of his unexpected liberation lay in the possibility of a journey which D. had been vaguely planning ever since the genius of Spontini had been revealed to him. To hear *La Vestale* in Paris had become the fixed goal of his ambition.

The hour of reaching this goal was at hand, when an incident that our enthusiast could not foresee threw a hurdle in his path. Though born with a fiery character and unconquerable passions, Adolphe was nevertheless shy in the presence of women, and apart from some less than poetic affairs with the princesses of the theater, love, all-devouring love, frantic love, the only love that could seem genuine to him, had not yet dug a crater in his heart. On returning home one evening, he found the following note:

Sir,

    If you should find it possible to devote a few hours to the musical education of a pupil who is already sufficiently advanced not to put too great a strain on your patience, I should be glad if you would place them at my disposal. Your talents are better known and better appreciated than perhaps you yourself suspect, so you must not be surprised if immediately on her arrival in your city, a Parisian woman hastens to charge you with the direction of her studies in the great art which you honor and thoroughly understand.

Hortense N.

Death by Enthusiasm

This blend of flattery and self-conceit, the tone at once detached and engaging, aroused D.'s curiousity so that instead of answering the letter, he decided to call on the Parisian lady herself, thank her for her expression of confidence, assure her that she in no way "surprised" him, and inform her that, being on the point of leaving for Paris, he could not undertake the unquestionably agreeable task that she proposed.

This little speech, rehearsed beforehand with the appropriate irony, expired on his lips the moment he entered the stranger's sitting-room. The unusual and challenging grace of Hortense, her deftly fashionable mode of dress, the something indefinable that is so fascinating in the gait and carriage and all the movements of a beauty from the Chaussée d'Antin, made their impact on Adolphe. Instead of irony, he began to utter regrets at his approaching departure. The tone of his voice, the dismay visible in his features gave proof of his sincerity, but Mme. N., like a clever woman, interrupted him:

"You are leaving? Then I was well advised to lose no time. You are going to Paris, but let us begin our lessons during the few days that remain. As soon as the cure season in your city is over, I am going back to the capital, where I shall be charmed to see you again and take further advantage of your instruction."

Adolphe, secretly happy to see his arguments for refusing so easily disposed of, promised to begin the next day and left the house in a dream. That day he did not give one thought to *La Vestale*.

Mme N. was one of those adorable women (as they say at the Café de Paris, Tortoni's, and three or four of the other resorts of dandyism) who find their slightest whims "delightfully novel," and feel that it would be tantamount to murder not to gratify them. They profess a species of respect for their own fancies, however absurd they are.

"My dear Fr—" said one of these charming creatures to a celebrated dilettante a few years ago, "you know Rossini: tell him from me that his *William Tell* is a deadly thing, it is enough to bore one to extinction; he must *not* take it into his head to write a second opera in that vein—otherwise Mme M. and I, who have always given him our support, will abandon him to his fate." And on another occasion: "Who on earth is this new Polish pianist whom all you artists are so crazy about and whose music is so queer? I want to see him; bring him around tomorrow."

"Madam, I will do my best, but I must confess that I am but slightly acquainted with him and that he is not mine to command."

"No, no, of course not; you can't issue an order, but he will obey mine, so I count on his coming."

This strange invitation not having been accepted, the queen told her subjects that M Chopin was "an odd little body," who played the piano "passably well," but that his music was simply "one long riddle, a ridiculous acrostic."

A fancy of this sort was the main motive behind the rather impertinent note that Adolphe had received from Mme N. as he was preparing to leave for Paris. The beautiful Hortense was a most accomplished pianist and gifted with the magnificent voice which she used as well as it is possible to do when the soul is not in it. She therefore stood in no need of the lessons of the Provençal musician. But his shouting defiance to the public in the theater had had reverberations throughout the town, and our Parisian lady, hearing them talked about on all sides, obtained particulars about the hero of an adventure which seemed to her full of piquancy.

She too "wanted to have him brought around," fully intending, after she had ascertained at leisure what sort of "odd little body" he was, and after she had played with him and upon him as on a new instrument, to send him about his business for good.

But matters turned out quite differently, much to the annoyance of the pretty *Simia parisiensis*. Adolphe was very handsome. Great black eyes full of flame, regular features, which a habitual pallor invested with a slight tinge of melancholy, but into which the warmest color came from time to time as enthusiasm or indignation quickened his pulse; a distinguished bearing, and manners rather different from what might have been expected from someone who had seen almost nothing of the world except through the curtainhole of his theater; a character at

Death by Enthusiasm

once passionate and reserved, with the most singular mixture of stiffness and grace, brusqueness and forebearance, sudden gaiety and deep abstraction—such traits made him, by their unexpectedness, the man most capable of catching a coquette in her own net.

And that is just what happened, though without premeditation on Adolphe's part, for he was smitten before she was. From the very first lesson Mme N.'s musical mastery shone forth in all its splendor. Far from needing advice, she was in a position to give some to her new teacher. The sonatas of Steibelt—the Hummel of the day—the arias of Paisiello and Cimarosa, which she smothered with ornaments that were often original and daring, gave her an opportunity to make each facet of her talent sparkle in turn. Adolphe, to whom such a woman and so fine an execution were something new, soon fell completely under her spell. After Steibelt's grand fantasia, "The Storm," in which Hortense seemed to him to display all the powers of musical art, he said to her, trembling with emotion: "Madam, you were making fun of me when you asked me to give you lessons. But how could I take it amiss when your hoax has opened to my unsuspecting eyes the portals of the world of poetry, the artistic paradise of my dreams, turning these dreams into a dazzling reality? Please prolong the hoax, madam, I implore you—tomorrow, next day, every day. I shall be indebted to you for the most intoxicating joys it has ever been given to me to know."

The tone in which these words were spoken, the tears which welled up in his eyes, the nervous spasm which shook his frame, astonished Hortense even more that her talent had surprised the young artist. If, on the one hand, the arpeggios, the turns, the showy harmonies, the finely chopped melodies, that rippled from the hands of the graceful fairy caused, so to speak, a paralysis of amazement in Adolphe; on the other, his impressionable nature, his lively sensibility, the picturesque expressions he used, their very exaggeration, affected Hortense no less powerfully.

His impassioned praise, springing from true artistic bliss, was such a far cry from the lukewarm and studied approval of the dandies of Paris that self-esteem alone would have sufficed to make her look indulgently upon a man less outwardly favored than our hero. Art and enthusiasm were face to face for the first time; the result of the encounter was easy to foresee: Adolphe, drunk with love, seeking neither to conceal nor to moderate the impetus of his altogether southern passion, disconcerted Hortense completely, and thus unwittingly upset the plan of defense prepared by the coquette. It was all so new to her! Though not actually feeling anything like the devouring ardor of her lover, she nevertheless understood that here was a whole world of sensations (not to say emotions) that the insipidity of her earlier affairs had never disclosed.

They were thus both happy, each in his own way, for a few weeks. The departure for Paris, as may be imagined, was postponed indefinitely. Music was to Adolphe an echo of his profound happiness, the mirror in which were reflected the rays of his frenzied passion, whence they returned more scorching to his heart. To Hortense, on the contrary, music was but a relaxation about which she had long been blasé. It procured her some agreeable diversions, and the pleasure of shining in the eyes of her lover was often the only motive that could bring her to the piano.

Wholly given over to his rage for loving, Adolphe had during the first few days partly forgotten the fanaticism that had filled his life until then. Though far from sharing Mme N.'s sometimes strange opinions about the merits of the various works in her repertory, he nonetheless made extraordinary concessions to her, avoiding in their conversations without quite knowing why, the broaching of the musical doctrine. A vague instinct warned him that the divergence between them would have been too great. Nothing less than some frightful blasphemy, such as the one that had made him show the door to one of his pupils, could have upset the balance in Adolphe's heart between his violent love and his despotically impassioned artistic convictions. And this blasphemy, one day, did escape Hortense's pretty lips.

It was on a fine morning in the autumn. Adolphe, lying at his mistress's feet, was reveling in the melancholy happiness, the delightful dejection, that follows the great climaxes of voluptuous bliss. The atheist himself, in such moments, hears within himself a hymn of gratitude rising toward the unknown cause that gave him life. And at the same moment, death—

Death by Enthusiasm

a death "dreamy and calm as night," in Moore's beautiful words—is the goal earnestly desired, the only fitting one that our eyes, dimmed with celestial tears, can glimpse as the gift to crown that superhuman intoxication. The common life, life devoid of poetry and love, *prose* life, in which one walks instead of flying, speaks instead of singing, in which so many bright-colored flowers lack perfume and grace, in which genius is worshipped for a day or done glacial homage to, in which art is too often the partner of a misalliance, *this* life, in short, shows itself under so gloomy an aspect, feels so empty, that death, even stripped of the real charm it holds for a man drowned in happiness, would still seem desirable to him, by offering him an assured refuge from the insipid existence he above all things dreads.

Lost in thoughts of this kind, Adolphe was holding one of the delicate hands of his lady-love, imprinting on every finger slight nibbles which he effaced with endless kisses, while Hortense with her free hand, humming the while, ruffled the black locks of her lover. Hearing that voice, so pure, so full of seduction, he felt an irresistible impulse to ask: "Oh, do sing me the elegy in *La Vestale*, my love; you know the one I mean:

"Thou whom I leave on earth,
Mortal I dare not name.

"Sung by you, that inspired melody will be incredibly sublime. I can't imagine why I haven't asked you before. Sing, sing Spontini to me; let me enjoy every kind of happiness all at once."

"Really? Is that what you would like?" replied Mme N., with a slight pout she thought charming. "You *enjoy* that long, monotonous dirge? It's the most boring thing—like monks chanting! Still, if you insist—"

The cold blade of a dagger plunging into Adolphe's heart would not have lacerated it more cruelly than her words. Starting up like a man who discovers an unclean animal in the grass he has been sitting on, he first riveted on Hortense a dark glance full of threatening fire. Then, striding restlessly about the room, fists clenched, teeth convulsively set, he seemed to be taking counsel with himself about the way in which he should speak to signify their breaking off. To forgive such a remark was impossible. Love and admiration had fled, the angel had become an ordinary woman; the superior artist had fallen to the level of the ignorant and superficial amateurs who want art to "amuse them," never suspecting that it has a nobler mission. Hortense was now but a graceful form without mind or soul; the musician had nimble fingers and a warbler's throat, nothing more.

In spite of the torments Adolphe felt at his discovery, in spite of the horror of so abrupt a disenchantment, he would not have been likely to fail in consideration and tact when breaking off with a woman whose sole crime, after all, was to have perceptions inferior to his own and to love the pretty without understanding the beautiful. But as Hortense was not able to credit the violence of the storm she had just raised, the sudden contraction of Adolphe's features, his excited striding about the sitting-room, his barely controlled indignation—all this seemed to her so comical that she could not restrain a burst of mad merriment and she let out a peal of strident laughter.

Have you ever noticed how hateful a high crackling laugh can be in certain women? To me it seems the sure sign of a withered heart, selfishness, and coquetry. Just as the expression of great joy is in some women marked by charm and modesty, so in others it takes on a tone of indecent sarcasm. Their voice becomes harsh, impudent, and shameless, which is all the more odious the younger and prettier the woman is. At such times I can understand the pleasure of murdering, and I absent-mindedly reach for Othello's pillow. Adolphe no doubt had the same feelings in the matter. A moment before, he was already out of love with Mme N., but he had pity for her and her limited faculties; he would have left her coldly, but without insulting her. The stupid noise of her laughter, at the very instant when the wretched man felt his heart torn, exasperated him. A flash of hatred and unutterable contempt suddenly darted from his eyes. Wiping the cold perspiration from his brow with an angry gesture, he said in a voice she had never heard him use: "Madam, you are a fool."

That same evening he was on his way to Paris.

No one knows what the modern Ariadne thought on finding herself thus forsaken. At all events Bacchus, who was to console her and heal the cruel wound inflicted on her self-esteem, was probably not slow in making his appearance. Hortense was not the woman to stay moping. "Her mind and heart required sustenance." Such is the usual phrase with which such women poetize and try to justify their most prosaic lapses from grace.

Be that as it may, from the second day of his journey, Adolphe had completely broken the spell and was all wrapped up in the joy of seeing his darling hope, his obsessive dream, on the verge of realization. At last he was to see Paris, to be in the center of the musical world. He was about to hear the magnificent orchestra of the Paris Opéra, with its large and powerful chorus, he would see Mme Branchu in *La Vestale*. A review by Geoffroy, which he read on reaching Lyon, further increased his impatience. Contrary to custom, the famous critic had uttered nothing but praise.

"Never," he wrote, "had Spontini's beautiful score been given with such fine ensemble by orchestra and chorus, nor with such passionate inspiration by the principal actors. Mme Branchu, among others, soared to the highest pitch of tragedy; a finished singer, gifted with an incomparable voice, a consummate actress, she is perhaps the most valuable member that the Opéra has been able to boast of since the day of its foundation—be it said with due deference to the admirers of Mme Saint-Huberty. Mme Branchu is, unfortunately, small in stature; but the naturalness of her attitudes, the energetic truth of her gestures, and the fire in her eyes make this lack of stature pass unnoticed. In her exchanges with the priests of Jupiter her acting is so expressive that she seems to tower a full head above Dérivis, who is a colossus.

"Last night a very long intermission preceded the third act. The reason for this unusual pause in the performance was the violent state of excitement into which the part of Julia and Spontini's music had thrown the singer. In the prayer ('O ye unfortunates') her tremulous voice already betrayed an emotion she could scarcely control, but in the finale ('Of this temple priestess lost in sin'), her part being all pantomime and not requiring her to restrain so completely the transports that agitated her, tears flooded her checks, her gestures became disordered, incoherent, wild; and when the pontiff threw over her head the huge black veil which covers her like a shroud, instead of fleeing distracted, as she had always done before, Mme Branchu dropped fainting at the feet of the Grand Vestal. The public, mistaking this for a new invention by the actress, covered with applause the peroration of this magnificent finale. Chorus, orchestra, Dérivis, the gong—all was drowned out by the shouts of the audience. The house was in a state of frenzy."

"My kingdom for a horse!" exclaimed Richard III. Adolphe would have given the whole world to have been able to gallop from Lyon to Paris then and there. He could hardly breathe as he read Geoffroy's words. The blood throbbed in his head and made him deaf, he was in a fever. Perforce he had to wait till the starting-time of the lumbering coach, so inappropriately called a diligence, in which he had reserved a seat for the next day.

During his few hours in Lyon, Adolphe took good care not to enter a theater. On any other occasion he would have been eager to do so; but feeling sure as he now did that he would soon hear Spontini's masterpiece worthily performed, he wished to remain until then virginally pure of all contact with the provincial Muses.

At last they were off. Ensconced in a corner of the carriage, buried in thought, D. maintained an unsociable silence and took no part in the cackling of three ladies who were taking pains to keep up a steady conversation with a couple of soldiers. The talk, as usual, ran on every conceivable subject, and when the turn of music came, the thousand and one absurdities retailed barely drew from Adolphe the laconic aside: "Old hens!" But the next day he was forced to answer the questions that the eldest of the women was determined to ask him. All three of them had lost patience with his persistent silence and the sardonic smile that played from time to time on his features. They made up their minds that he should speak and tell them the object of his journey.

"You are no doubt going to Paris?"

"Yes, madam."

"To study law?"

Death by Enthusiasm

"No, madam."

"Ah, then, you are a medical student?"

"Not at all, madam."

The questioning had come to an end for the time being. It was resumed the next day with an importunity fit to make the most forbearing man lose patience.

"Can it be that our young friend is about to enter the Polytechnic School?"

"No, madam."

"Some business firm, then?"

"Heavens, no, madam."

"As a matter of fact, nothing is nicer than to travel for pleasure, as you appear to be doing."

"That may have been my object in setting out, madam, but I am doomed to miss it altogether, if the future is anything like the present."

This rejoinder, dryly uttered, had the effect of silencing the impertinent questioner at last, and Adolphe was able to take up the thread of his thoughts. How was he going to manage in Paris? His whole fortune consisted of his violin and a purse containing two hundred francs. By what means could he put the former to use and save the contents of the latter? Would he find a way to make something of his talent? But what matter all these worries about trifles and fears about the future? Was he not going to hear *La Vestale*? Was he not on the point of enjoying to its fullest the happiness so long dreamed of? Even if he should die the moment after, he would have no complaint. It was in truth perfectly fair that life should come to an end when the sum of the possible joys that fill a human existence is spent at one stroke.

In his state of exaltation our Provençal reached Paris. Hardly out of the carriage, he rushed to look at the playbills. But what does he see on the Opéra's: *The Betrothed*! "A barefaced fraud!" he exclaims; "what was the use of getting myself expelled from my theater and flying from Lemoyne's music as from plague and leprosy, only to find it again at the Paris Opéra?"

The fact is that this mongrel work, this archetype of the powdered, embroidered, gold-laced rococo style, which seems to have been composed expressly for the Viscount Jodelet and the Marquis de Mascarille, was then in high favor. Lemoyne shared the programs in alteration with Gluck and Spontini. In Adolphe's eyes the putting of these names cheek by jowl was a desecration. It seemed to him that a stage adorned by the finest geniuses of Europe should not be open to such pallid mediocrities; that the noble orchestra, still vibrating with the virile tones of *Iphigenia in Tauris* or *Alcestis*, should not be debased by having to accompany the twitterings of Mondor and la Dandinière. As for the comparison between *La Vestale* and those ghastly and stale potpourris, he tried to drive the thought from his mind. Such an abomination curdled his blood, and to this day there still exist a few ardent or *extravagant* minds (you may call them either way) who take exactly the same view of the matter.

Swallowing his disappointment, Adolphe was glumly going home when chance made him meet a fellow countryman to whom he had formerly given lessons. The latter, a wealthy amateur and well known in musical circles, readily told his former teacher all he knew about what was going on, and reported that the performances of *La Vestale*, which had been suspended because of Mme Branchu's indisposition, would in all probability not be resumed for some weeks to come. As for Gluck's works, which ordinarily formed the core of the Opéra's repertory, they were not scheduled during the first days of Adolphe's stay in Paris. This circumstance made it easier for him to fulfill the vow he had made of preserving his musical virginity for Spontini. He did not set foot in any theater and abstained from every kind of music.

Meanwhile he sought a position that would give him his daily bread without condemning him anew to the humiliating role he had so long occupied in the provinces. He played to Persuis, at that time conductor at the Opéra. Persuis saw that he had talent, invited him to come and see him again, and promised him the first opening among the violins of the Opéra. Thus reassured, and banking for his livelihood on a couple of pupils whom his patron had found for him, the worshipper at Spontini's shrine felt increasing impatience to hear the magic score. Every day he ran out to scan the playbills, only to have his hopes dashed to the ground.

On the morning of the 22nd of March, reaching the corner of the rue Richelieu just as the

Death by Enthusiasm

billposter was climbing up his ladder, and seeing the placard of, successively, the Vaudeville, the Opéra-Comique, the Italian Theater, and the Porte-Saint-Martin, finally saw the slow unfolding of the large brown sheet bearing as headline the words "*Académie impériale de Musique.*" He nearly collapsed in the street on reading at last the title so greatly desired: *La Vestale.*

Hardly had Adolphe seen this promise of *La Vestale* for the next day when he was seized by a sort of delirium. He rushed madly through the streets, bumping into the jutting angles of houses, elbowing passers-by, laughing at their insults, talking, singing, gesticulating like an escaped lunatic.

Dead with fatigue, spattered with mud, he finally entered a café, ordered dinner, wolfed down without noticing what the waiter set before him, and lapsed into a strange fit of melancholy. Suddenly a prey to anxiety without quite discerning what could be causing it, and over-awed by the nearness of the stupendous event which was to come into his life, he listened awhile to the violent thumping of his heart, he wept, and letting his poor, emaciated head drop to the table, he fell into a deep sleep.

The following day he was calmer. A call on Persuis shortened his wait. The manager, on receiving Adolphe, handed him a letter bearing the official stamp of the Opéra: it was his appointment as second violin. Adolphe thanked him, though with much alacrity. This favor, which at any other time would have overwhelmed him with joy, had become to him hardly more than a secondary matter of little interest. A few minutes later he had forgotten it. He avoided speaking to Persuis of the performance that was to take place that evening; the subject would have shaken him to the core. He dreaded it. Persuis, not knowing what to think of the young man's strange looks and incoherent speech, was about to ask the cause of the trouble, when Adolphe noticed this, rose and left.

He strolled awhile in front of the Opéra, looked again at the bill to make sure there was no change in the program or in the cast. All this helped him to wait till the close of that interminable day. At last the clock struck six. Twenty minutes later Adolphe was in his box, for in order to be undisturbed in his ecstatic admiration, and to enhance the solemnity of his happiness, he had taken, regardless of the extravagant expenditure, and entire box for himself alone.

We shall now let our enthusiast give his own account of that memorable evening. A few lines that he wrote on reaching home, as a sequel to the sort of diary from which I have culled the foregoing particulars, show but too well the state of his mind and the inconceivable frenzy which formed the groundwork of his temperament. I give them here without alteration.

"March 23rd, midnight

"This, then, is life! I gaze upon it from the pinnacle of my happiness . . . it is impossible to go further. . . . I have reached the summit. . . . Come down again? Go back? . . . Certainly not! I prefer making my exit before nauseating tastes poison that of the delicious fruit I have just plucked. What would my life be if it were to go on?—that of the thousands of insects I hear buzzing about me. Chained once more to a music-stand, forced to play in alternation masterpieces and filthy platitudes, I should end like the rest and become hardened. The exquisite sensibility that enables me to enjoy so many sensations and gives me access to so many emotions unknown to the common herd would gradually become blunted, and my enthusiasm would cool, even supposing it did not die out altogether under the ashes of habit. I might perhaps come to speak of geniuses as if they were ordinary beings; I might utter the names of Gluck and Spontini without raising my hat. I am fairly sure that I should always hate with all my soul anything I now hate; but is it not a cruel necessity to husband one's energy only for the purposes of hatred?

"Music occupies too large a place in my life. My passion for it has killed and absorbed all the rest. My last experience of love has disillusioned me only too harshly. Could I ever find a woman whose being would be tuned to the same high pitch as mine? No, I'm afraid they are all more or less like Hortense. I had forgotten her name—Hortense—odd how a single word from her mouth broke the spell! Oh, the humiliation of having loved with the most ardent and poetic love, with all the strength of my heart and soul, a woman possessed of neither, and

Death by Enthusiasm

radically incapable of understanding the meaning of the words "love" and "poetry." Fool, thrice-silly fool, of whom I still cannot think without a blush.

"Yesterday I thought of writing to Spontini and begging him to let me pay a call. But even if my request had been granted, the great man would never have believed me capable of understanding his work as I do understand it. I should probably appear to him merely as an excited young man, childishly infatuated with a work miles above his grasp. He would think of me what he must necessarily think of the public. He might even attribute my transports of admiration to shameful self-interest, thus confusing the most sincere enthusiasm with the meanest flattery. Horrible! No, no, better make an end of it. I am alone in the world, an orphan from childhood; my death will grieve no one. A few will say: 'He was crazy.' That will be my epitaph.

"I shall die day after tomorrow. *La Vestale* is to be performed again, I want to hear it a second time. What a work! How love is pictured in it! as well as fanaticism! All those mastiff-priests barking at their wretched victim! And what harmonies in that gigantic finale! What melody even in the recitatives! What an orchestra! It moves so majestically; the basses swell and sink like the waves of the ocean. The instruments are actors whose language is as expressive as that spoken on the stage. Dérivis was superb in his recitative of the second act: he was *Jupiter Tonans*. In the aria "Unrelenting gods," Mme Branchu tore my heart out; I nearly fainted. That woman is lyric tragedy incarnate; she would reconcile me to her sex. Yes! I shall see her again . . . once . . . this *Vestale* . . . a superhuman work, which could have come to birth only in an age of miracles like Napoleon's. I shall focus into three hours the life force of twenty years' existence. Afterwards, I shall go . . . and ponder over my happiness in eternity."

Two days later, at ten o'clock at night, a report was heard at the corner of the rue Rameau, opposite the entrance to the Opéra. Some footmen in gorgeous liveries rushed to the spot on hearing the noise, and raised the body of a man bathed in blood who showed no signs of life. At that instant a lady who was leaving the theater came to find her carriage and recognizing the blood-bespattered face of Adolphe, said: "Oh, mercy! It's that unhappy young man who's been following me all the way from Marseille!"

Hortense (for it was she) had then and there seen the way to make her vanity benefit from the death of the man who had vexed her by his humiliating departure. The next day the talk in the club in the rue de Choiseul was: "That Mme N. is really a captivating woman! When she went south time ago, a Provençal fell so madly in love with her that he followed her all the way to Paris and blew his brains out at her feet last night, just outside the Opéra. That's success, as you might say; it will make her absolutely irresistible."

Poor Adolphe! . . .

Death by Enthusiasm

Butterfly's Failure

George R. Marek

Even Giacomo Puccini had his bad nights. The maestro's biographer Marek calls the mysterious opening-night bomb of Madama Butterfly, *"one of the most spectacular scandals in operatic history." His account of Puccini's disaster opens a window on backstage intrigue La Scala–style.*

*B*utterfly was offered to La Scala—and promptly accepted. It was understood that La Scala, under the management of Giulio Gatti-Casazza, would give the opera the finest possible production. The scenery was designed in Paris by the famous stage designer Jusseaume. Giovanni Zenatello was Pinkerton, Giuseppe de Luca Sharpless, the conductor Campanini. And Cio-Cio-San was Rosina Storchio, a superb singer and a beautiful woman, small, delicate, intelligent, sensitive to direction, young, and suffused with artistic sincerity. All who worked with her remember her affectionately and speak of her with smiling admiration. She was one of Toscanini's favorite singers. In short, the cast, as Gatti-Casazza says in his *Memories of Opera*, was "ideal."

Puccini was confident. He had completed the music at a time when he had been an invalid and suffering pain. But of invalidism, he knew, there was no trace in the score. He had given of his best. Confined to the wheelchair, he had refined the music in the crucible of concentration. He had worked over every passage, correcting and improving countless times, as the manuscript shows. He loved Cio-Cio-San, this child of a strange country, more than he had loved any of his previous heroines. "There is no comparison," he said, "between my love for

Mimi, Musetta, Manon, and Tosca and that love which I have in my heart for her for whom I wrote music in the night . . ." During the rehearsals at La Scala, over which Tito Ricordi presided, the stagehands, men not easily impressed, walked on tiptoe, often stopped their work altogether, and listened with tears in their eyes. After the dress rehearsal, the orchestra rose to its feet and congratulated the composer with the greatest sincerity. Yes, for once there was no doubt about it: this was going to be a success. Puccini always begged his family to stay away from his premieres. This was the one and only time that he not only permitted them to come but actually invited his sisters to Milan. At the beginning of the performance, three of them, decorously clad in black, were to be seen ensconced in a box.

Expectation was enormous. Admission prices were raised. Twenty-five thousand lire were taken in at the box office, a record. On the day of the performance, Puccini sent Rosina Storchio a note:

February 17, 1904

DEAREST ROSINA:

My good wishes are not necesssary. So true, so fine, so moving is your wonderful art that the public must succumb to it! I hope that through you I will gain my victory. Until tonight, then—with confidence and much affection.

The night came. The audience assembled. The curtain rose. The beginning of the opera, up to the entrance of Butterfly, was heard in silence. An ominous sign, for Italian audiences do not listen in silence when they like what they are hearing. Just before the entrance of Butterfly— Storchio was standing in the wings with Puccini, her hands cold as ice—a super came by mumbling, "What is the matter with the public?" Storchio broke out into a cold sweat. The assistant conductor pointed: it was her cue. She sang backstage the first phrase of Cio-Cio-San's, that enchanting phrase, "One more step and we have arrived." She was on the stage. Silence. No applause. She continued to sing. And suddenly there was a shout from the balcony, "That is

Bohème." Immediately the cry was echoed by other voices: "*Bohème! Bohème!* We've heard that already. Give us something new!" Then all was quiet again. Quiet during the wedding ceremony. Quiet during the long love duet. At the climax of the duet a few handclaps; so sparse were they that in the darkness of the theater they sounded like an emphasis on silence. The curtain fell. Again a little applause—very little—mixed with the hisses. There were three curtain calls, in two of which the reluctant Puccini, leaning on his cane, participated.

During the first intermission, no one came backstage, not a friend, not a journalist. An actor once told me that failure could always be recognized after the first act. If no one appeared to make a fuss over you, you were ready to look for another job. There were two hectic spots on Puccini's face as he walked up and down, smoking one cigarette after another, unmindful of the two firemen stationed backstage. Tito Ricordi was cold and composed. He went over to Storchio and said, "At the second act the reaction will set in. I swear to you that it will be a success."

The second act began. At one moment Storchio turned around quickly. A draft caught her kimono and it ballooned up. At that a hoarse voice in the audience shouted, "Butterfly is pregnant." Storchio began to weep. She finished "*Un bel dì*" in a voice thickened by tears. There was again scattered applause. But when she introduced the child to Sharpless, pandemonium broke loose. Grunts, growls, groans, laughter, ironic cries of "*Bis!*," obscene remarks, hisses hailed down on the performers. From then on hardly a note was heard in silence. The derogatory noises reached their climax during the Intermezzo. (We must remember that *Butterfly* in the original version was given in two acts, the Intermezzo connecting Scenes I and 2 of Act II.) Tito had had the unfortunate idea of reinforcing the effect of the music by producing from hidden parts of the auditorium itself the gentle chirping of birds. As the sky darkened and night fell, as Butterfly, Suzuki, and child stood looking out over the landscape, these aviary twitterings were to be heard. A tasteless bit of realism, which gave a cue to the audience. They answered: they barked like dogs, burst into cock-a-doodle-doos of roosters, brayed like asses, and mooed like cows as if—Storchio said—dawn in Japan were taking place in

Noah's Ark. Nothing after that failed to strike the audience as funny. The final scene, the preparation for the suicide and the suicide itself, was heard in comparative quiet, but when the curtain fell, *Butterfly* ended amidst laughter and derogatory shouts. There were no curtain calls, not a single one.

Long before the opera ended, the composer's son Tonio had come backstage. The boy hurled himself into the arms of Puccini, crying, "Oh, Father! Father!" Puccini hid in one of the dressing rooms, but the furor and the noise reached him there also. He heard "those whistles, those terrible whistles, which humiliate you, which slap you down, which tear your heart into pieces. . . . How is it possible that the public, even if the work be a mistake, can be so ferocious; how is it possible that it cannot pity, that it cannot consider that behind the scenery on that stage there stands an artist who has attempted to create something, a father who loves his work and who suffers to see it tortured, offended, abused? Good people, one by one, the spectators. But together, once out for evil, they are rabble."

Puccini slunk home. He had not far to go: his apartment in the Via Verdi was across the street from the Scala. Even these few steps were painful: he hid himself against the walls as if—he said—he had been a man who had committed a dirty crime. He could not understand. As he sat with Elvira, Tito, and Giulio through a sleepless night, he demanded to know how it could have happened that he, who thought himself loved, if not by all, certainly by many, could now be "one against the crowd, defenseless, at the mercy of a furious audience who turned into ridicule the opera born in the deepest recesses of my heart. . . . My whole life passed before me. There were some things beyond the ken of the public's judgment of one night. . . . And I determined that *Madama Butterfly*, however miserably it might have fallen when it took the first step, should not stop here at the Scala of Milan, but would continue its way in the world. . . . I thought of Bellini, remembering the enormous fiasco at the Scala [of *Norma*]; I thought of the cries which met Rossini at the first performance of *The Barber*; I thought of Wagner and the sounds of the hunting horns blown by the Parisian aristocrats who drowned his *Tannhäuser* in ridicule. . . ."

Then other friends came in and Puccini turned to them in a burst of unjust anger: "Have you too whistled at my opera? Did you too shout? Do as you like. I know what I have accomplished, even if the others do not. *Butterfly* is my best opera." After this he became calmer.

His humiliation was not over. Morning came and with it the cries of the newsboys. In his apartment he could not shut out the sounds of those headlines. Of all of them—"BUTTERFLY A FAILURE," "PUCCINI HISSED," "FIASCO AT THE SCALA," etc.—the one which hurt him most was "BUTTERFLY DIABETIC OPERA, RESULT OF AUTOMOBILE ACCIDENT."

There is no question but that the disgraceful scene in the theater had been organized. This was not spontaneous disapproval. It was a deliberate affront, engineered and staged. Ricordi's statements, made after the premiere, and other evidence leave no doubt on the matter. Ricordi said:

> After this pandemonium, throughout which practically nothing could be heard, the public left the theater as pleased as Punch. And one had never before seen so many happy, or such joyously satisfied faces—satisfied as if by a triumph in which all had shared. In the atrium of the theater the joy was at its height, and there were those who rubbed their hands, underlining the gesture with the solemn words, *Consummatum est, parce sepulto!* The performance given in the pit seems to have been as well organized as that on the stage, since it too began punctually with the beginning of the opera. This is the true account of the evening.

Colombo, Sr., who was at the time working for Ricordi and later became the manager of the firm, told me that he had worked for weeks to make sure that the piano scores of *Butterfly* were available in the music stores of Milan on the day of the performance. They were displayed in all the shop windows. The day after, every one of these scores disappeared. This could not have been done, he said, except through concerted action on the part of a clique working together.

Who was this clique? Who were the people who set into motion one of the most spectacular scandals in operatic history? We shall never know precisely. We shall not be able to name the instigators, unless documents come to the surface. This is most unlikely, as intrigues of this kind are not documented. Knowing Italian operatic life, we can guess that the group consisted of rival composers and their adherents, the same group, probably, who had planned to threaten the first performance of *Tosca*. Not much love was lost between Puccini and his colleagues. He held himself apart. He did not fraternize with the crowd that visited the Galleria in Milan and frequented the salons. He was too outspoken in his opinion of contemporary Italian music. More important, he was now so ubiquitously popular that a check to his career seemed a necessary measure. Puccini himself said that "there were people there who for years had waited for the joy of laying me low—at whatever cost."

But even a well-organized faction could hardly have produced the result they did, if the nonprofessional audience at the Scala had genuinely enjoyed the opera. The audience did *not* enjoy it. Even spectators of good will could hardly have done so. After the first outcries of the troublemakers, the opera's spell was broken. Puccini said that *Butterfly* was "a work of suggestion. Once the suggestion was breached, the magic faded." But there was another reason. *Butterfly* was, in its original version, not nearly so stageworthy a work as it is now. Mosco Carner has made a special study of the original and the revised scores. The revisions, he says in *Of Men and Music*, at first glance do not seem to amount to much; "but on closer examination, most of them are found to be important and necessary." There were only two acts, making each act of a greater length than the Italian public was used to. "For once, Puccini's unfailing sense for the balance of acts failed completely; for not only was there a striking disproportion between the lengths of the first and second acts—the former lasting about fifty-five minutes, the latter about ninety minutes—but the second in itself was too long."

There is very little action of any kind in the first act of the opera except the wedding ceremony. And that wedding ceremony was presented in tiresome detail. Butterfly's relatives were introduced, Japanese refreshments were served, and Pinkerton commented on them.

Butterfly's Failure

This was followed by an episode in which Butterfly's uncle, Yakusidé, got drunk. Puccini shortened the scene in the revision.

In the second act, the scene of Butterfly's make-up was too dragged out. Moreover, in the original version it was Kate Pinkerton who asked Butterfly for the child, at the very moment when Cio-Cio-San realizes that Pinkerton has betrayed her. This, says Carner, "was a piece of most sadistic cruelty and utter tastelessness withall." He concludes: "In comparing the two versions on paper, the difference may not seem very striking. But on the stage, with its subtle laws of weight, balance, timing, and 'spacing' of scenes, Puccini's revisions went a long way. They most probably saved the work from remaining a 'near miss.'" Giuseppe de Luca confirmed this opinion. He told me that in performance the difference between the two versions was considerable.

On the morning of the eighteenth, Puccini held a meeting at his apartment at which were present Tito and Giulio Ricordi, Illica and Giacosa—and Rosina Storchio. The following decisions were taken: (1) The opera was to be withdrawn immediately. The second performance, already announced, was to be canceled. (2) The composer's, the librettists', and Ricordi's share in the proceeds of the performance were to be restituted to the management of La Scala. This was a heroic gesture: the sum involved was twenty thousand lire. (3) Puccini was to withdraw the score from general circulation, canceling also a projected performance in Rome, and he was to revise it, dividing the opera into three acts. (4) The revisions completed, the opera was to be given in its new version not in Milan but in a smaller theater as a tryout.

Under the circumstances, a calm, critical appraisal of the opera was impossible. Giovanni Pozza, of the *Corriere della Sera*, was the most sympathetic of the critics. He found much fault with the work, calling attention to "details which were too minute," and with the action, which was "uselessly repeated and prolix." But he also found much beauty in the music, and ended his article with, "The opera did not pass the test. All the same, I persist in believing that this work, abbreviated and lightened, will rise again. Scattered through it are too many beautiful pages, it is stamped with too much elegance and grace. Better to await, before pronouncing the final word, a judgment more calm and considered."

But Puccini's humiliation was even yet not complete. The fiasco was too good a subject for the newspapers to let go.

On the twentieth of February, *Il Secolo* carried an announcement concerning the withdrawal of the opera, "in spite of insistent protests by the management of the theater." (This was true: Gatti-Casazza liked the work and did not wish to withdraw it.) *Faust* was going to be substituted for the next performance. The article continued:

> It is easily understood that *Butterfly* could not be given again after the crushing result which *La Perseveranza* has frankly called a fiasco. A second performance would have provoked a scandal which would have called for decided action on the part of the Milanese public, who do not relish being mocked. This opera is not one of those, like *The Barber of Seville*, which carry in them the seeds of resurrection. It reveals that Maestro Puccini was in a hurry. Importuned as he was to bring out the work this season, sick as he was, he did not find original inspiration and took recourse to melodies from his previous operas, and even helped himself to melodies of other composers. In his defense we must say that the libretto was artistically unfortunate. . . . The opera is dead.

But perhaps because meanness was applied with so heavy a hand, a sense of justice and fairness began to spring up among the public. Voices were raised to defend the work. As early as the nineteenth of February, an anonymous letter appeared in the *Corriere della Sera*. It read in part:

> I am neither a critic nor a musician, but music may be enjoyed by anyone who possesses good, sensitive ears, and as to the theater, I understand it as anybody would who goes there frequently. This does not give me the right to voice my modest judgment

about *Butterfly* publicly. But there is one matter on which I do consider myself competent, and that is manners. Permit me to say, therefore, that while last night a performance of an opera took place which may or may not have been worthy of applause, in the audience something took place which lacked all courtesy. This Giacomo Puccini was, a few hours, before the curtain went up, the idol of the public. His melodies sound in all ears and are on all lips. . . . It sufficed that a new opera was given which did not please, to turn this favorite into more or less of a delinquent. A hunt of wild ferocity went on last night. Why? Did none of those people in the audience ever make a mistake? Are there no businessmen who mismanage an affair? Lawyers who lose a case? Engineers who miscalculate? And does a similar vindictive ire surge up at every error? A business deal, a lawsuit, a mathematical calculation are minor episodes. An opera is quite another matter, especially an opera by Puccini. . . . I witnessed disgusting scenes. There were people there who, at every attempt to applaud, wore an expression of atrocious suffering. So much so, that at a certain point I turned to a man who whimpered, roared, and sweated hatred from all pores, and said to him, "Puccini must have accomplished something if he made you that ferocious."

There are plenty of signs around prohibiting spitting on the floor. This is good for physical hygiene. Is nothing to be done for moral hygiene?

ONE OF THE PUBLIC

Puccini never forgot the seventeenth of February, 1904. For a long time it made him unsure of his own judgment. He no longer understood *Il Signor Pubblico*, he said. Particularly did he fear and distrust from now on the public of the Scala. Eventually the howl of the fiasco became dim, yet it never entirely ceased to sound in the dark background of his mind.

At the time, he was particularly friendly with two brothers, Ippolito and Camillo Bondi, music lovers both, who had been kind to him in his youth. The heirs of the Bondi family gave me the letters of Puccini written immediately after *Butterfly*.

[To Camillo]   MILAN, February 18, 1904

With a sad but strong heart I tell you that it was a lynching! Those cannibals didn't listen to one single note—what a terrible orgy of madmen drunk with hate! But my *Butterfly* remains as it is: the most felt and most expressive opera that I have conceived! I shall win in the end, you'll see—if it is given in a smaller theater, less permeated by hatred and passion. Here I have withdrawn the opera and refunded the money, in agreement with my collaborators; and I shall not give it in Rome if I can free myself of that contract, because I am sure that even there I would have trouble, as the atmosphere is not serene—and besides, I don't want to give it there! I shall give it in a smaller theater, in another city, where there is tranquility. Enough—You'll see if I am right.

[To Camillo]   MILAN, February 22, 1904

I am still shocked by all that happened—not so much for what they did to my poor *Butterfly*, but for the poison that they spat at me as an artist and as a man! And I can't explain why all this was done to me, who live far away from all human contacts. They have printed all kinds of things! Now they say that I am going to rewrite the opera and that it will take me six months! Nothing of the kind! I am not rewriting anything, or, at least, very few details—I shall make a few cuts and divide the second act in two—something which I had already thought of doing during the rehearsals, but it was then too near the first performance. . . . That performance was a Dantean Inferno, prepared in advance. . . .

[To Ippolito]   MILAN, February 22, 1904

The reaction of the public has begun here, and the fact that the opera was withdrawn after the first performance has made quite an impression. . . . I thank you from the bottom of my heart for your kind interest in me and my opera. Isn't it true that it is not the awful thing that every one (*I say every one*) of those cannibals said it was?

Butterfly's Failure

Puccini returned to Torre del Lago to make his corrections. Tito Ricordi, who had not lost faith in *Butterfly*, chose Brescia for the premiere of the revised version. This performance took place of the twenty-eighth of May, 1904, with Salomea Krucenisca as Butterfly (Storchio had gone to South America).

Brescia is near Milan. At any rate, the representatives of the Milan press could hardly have been prevented from coming to Brescia to find out what new excitement was in store. The performance, says Fraccaroli, seemed more like a first night at the Scala than a provincial opening. The curious and the sensation seekers were everywhere. Tension was high.

And yet how different were the results! At the very opening of the curtain, the scenery was applauded. The first small tenor aria was greeted with shouts of approval. The public insisted that it be repeated. Repeated it was, and Puccini had to bow on the stage. Thunders of applause at Butterfly's entrance. Once more Puccini had to show himself. During the love duet, the audience sat quiet. Here and there applause broke out but this was indignantly hushed—the spectators, provincial and cosmopolitan, wished to savor the music to the full. But at the climax, when Butterfly sang, "Sweet night, how many stars!" there came a clapping of hands so overwhelming that it covered voices and orchestra. The curtain fell, and then the audience really broke loose. Nothing would do but that the curtain had again to be raised and the entire love duet repeated! Friends, critics, composers—including Arrigo Boito—rushed backstage among a general hubbub of jubilation.

The excitement continued in the second act. Four numbers were encored: "*Un bel dì*," the reading of the letter, the flower duet, and the Intermezzo. Puccini had to appear ten times. Brescia did its best to compensate him for what had been done to him in Milan.

Not a soul went home at the end. They stood, they screamed, they waved, while over and over again Puccini bowed.

In the spring of that year, Toscanini took *Butterfly* to Buenos Aires. There, with Rosina Storchio in the part, it was as great a triumph as it had been in Brescia.

Never again did *Butterfly* fail. No other first performance proved short of a triumph.

George R. Marek

Within a few years it rivaled *Bohème* in popularity. Like *Bohème*, *Butterfly* evoked in opera-goers a feeling of special tenderness, a smiling personal affection. Everybody wanted to pet and be good to the little geisha girl—everybody, that is, who liked Puccini's music.

But like a father who cannot forget that his child has been a sickly infant, however sturdy he proves to be when he grows up, Puccini continued to regard the opera with sentimental anxiety. Rosina Storchio gave Puccini a painting of herself in the role. He hung this above his desk in the Via Verdi apartment. He looked at it often, and quoted the line from the opera, *"Rinnegata e felice"*—"Renounced but happy."

A Gold Slipper

Willa Cather

From her gown's provocative velvet train to her independent turn of mind, the visiting prima donna leaves a stolid coal magnate nonplussed—and, in spite of himself, infatuated.

M arshall McKann followed his wife and her friend Mrs. Post down the aisle and up the steps to the stage of the Carnegie Music Hall with an ill-concealed feeling of grievance. Heaven knew he never went to concerts, and to be mounted upon the stage in this fashion, as if he were a "highbrow" from Sewickley, or some unfortunate with a musical wife, was ludicrous. A man went to concerts when he was courting, while he was a junior partner. When he became a person of substance he stopped that sort of nonsense. His wife, too, was a sensible person, the daughter of an old Pittsburgh family as solid and well-rooted as the McKanns. She would never have bothered him about this concert had not the meddlesome Mrs. Post arrived to pay her a visit. Mrs. Post was an old school friend of Mrs. McKann, and because she lived in Cincinnati she was always keeping up with the world and talking about things in which no one else was interested, music among them. She was an aggressive lady, with weighty opinions, and a deep voice like a jovial bassoon. She had arrived only last night, and at dinner she brought it out that she could on no account miss Kitty Ayrshire's recital; it was, she said, the sort of thing no one could afford to miss.

When McKann went into town in the morning he found that every seat in the music-hall was sold. He telephoned his wife to that effect, and, thinking he had settled the matter, made his reservation on the 11:25 train for New York. He was unable to get a drawing-room because this same Kitty Ayrshire had taken the last one. He had not intended going to New York until the following week, but he preferred to be absent during Mrs. Post's incumbency.

In the middle of the morning, when he was deep in his correspondence, his wife called him up to say the enterprising Mrs. Post had telephoned some musical friends in Sewickley and had found that two hundred folding-chairs were to be placed on the stage of the concert-hall, behind the piano, and that they would be on sale at noon. Would he please get seats in the front row? McKann asked if they would not excuse him, since he was going over to New York on the late train, would be tired, and would not have time to dress, etc. No, not at all. It would be foolish for two women to trail up to the stage unattended. Mrs. Post's husband always accompanied her to concerts, and she expected that much attention from her host. He needn't dress, and he could take a taxi from the concert-hall to the East Liberty station.

The outcome of it all was that, though his bag was at the station, here was McKann, in the worst possible humor, facing the large audience to which he was well-known, and sitting among the lot of music students and excitable old maids. Only the desperately zealous or the morbidly curious would endure two hours in those wooden chairs, and he sat in the front row of this hectic body, somehow made a party to a transaction for which he had the utmost contempt.

When McKann had been in Paris, Kitty Ayrshire was singing at the Comique, and he wouldn't go to hear her—even there, where one found so little that was better to do. She was too much talked about, too much advertised; always being thrust in an American's face as if she were something to be proud of. Perfumes and petticoats and cutlets were named for her. Someone had pointed Kitty out to him one afternoon when she was driving in the Bois with a French composer—old enough, he judged, to be her father—who was said to be infatuated, carried away by her. McKann was told that this was one of the historic passions of old age. He had looked at her on that occasion, but she was so befrilled and befeathered that he

A Gold Slipper

caught nothing but a graceful outline and a small, dark head above a white ostrich boa. He had noted with disgust, however, the stooped shoulders and white imperial of the silk-hatted man beside her, and the senescent line of his back. McKann described to his wife this unpleasing picture only last night, while he was undressing, when he was making every possible effort to avert this concert party. But Bessie only looked superior and said she wished to hear Kitty Ayrshire sing, and that her "private life" was something in which she had no interest.

Well, here he was; hot and uncomfortable, in a chair much too small for him, with a row of blinding footlights glaring in his eyes. Suddenly the door at his right elbow opened. Their seats were at one end of the front row; he had thought they would be less conspicuous there than in the center, and he had not foreseen that the singer would walk over him every time she came upon the stage. Her velvet train brushed against his trousers as she passed him. The applause which greeted her was neither overwhelming nor prolonged. Her conservative audience did not know exactly how to accept her toilette. They were accustomed to dignified concert gowns, like those which Pittsburgh matrons (in those days!) wore at their daughters' coming-out teas.

Kitty's gown that evening was really quite outrageous—the repartée of a conscienceless Parisian designer who took her hint that she wished something that would be entirely novel in the States. Today, after we have all of us, even in the uttermost provinces, been educated by Bakst and the various Ballets Russes, we would accept such a gown without distrust; but then it was a little disconcerting, even to the well-disposed. It was constructed of a yard or two of green velvet—a reviling, shrieking green which would have made a fright of any woman who had not inextinguishable beauty—and it was made without armholes, a device to which we were then so unaccustomed that it was nothing less than alarming. The velvet skirt split back from a transparent gold-lace petticoat, gold stockings, gold slippers. The narrow train was, apparently, looped to both ankles, and it kept curling about her feet like a serpent's tail, turning up its gold lining as if it were squirming over on its back. It was not, we felt, a costume in which to sing Mozart and Handel and Beethoven.

Kitty sensed the chill in the air, and it amused her. She liked to be thought a brilliant artist by other artists, but by the world at large she liked to be thought a daring creature. She had every reason to believe, from experience and from example, that to shock the great crowd was the surest way to get its money and to make her name a household word. Nobody ever became a household word of being an artist, surely; and you were not a thoroughly paying proposition until your name meant something on the sidewalk and in the barbershop. Kitty studied her audience with an appraising eye. She liked the stimulus of this disapprobation. As she faced this hard-shelled public she felt keen and interested; she knew that she would give such a recital as cannot often be heard for money. She nodded gaily to the young man at the piano, fell into an attitude of seriousness, and began the group of Beethoven and Mozart songs.

Though McKann would not have admitted it, there were really a great many people in the concert-hall who knew what the prodigal daughter of their country was singing, and how well she was doing it. They thawed gradually under the beauty of her voice and the subtlety of her interpretation. She had sung seldom in concert then, and they supposed her very dependent upon the accessories of the opera. Clean singing, finished artistry, were not what they expected from her. They began to feel, even, the wayward charm of her personality.

McKann, who stared coldly up at the balconies during her first song, during the second glanced cautiously at the green apparition before him. He was vexed with her for having retained a debutante figure. He comfortably classed all singers—especially operatic singers—as "fat Dutchwomen" or "shifty Sadies," and Kitty would not fit into his clever generalization. She displayed, under his nose, the only kind of figure he considered worth looking at—that of a very young girl, supple and sinuous and quick-silverish; thin, eager shoulders, polished white arms that were nowhere too fat and nowhere too thin. McKann found it agreeable to look at Kitty, but when he saw that the authoritative Mrs. Post, red as a turkey-cock with opinions she was bursting to impart, was studying and appraising the singer through her lorgnette, he gazed indifferently out into the house again. He felt for his

A Gold Slipper

watch, but his wife touched him warningly with her elbow—which, he noticed, was not at all like Kitty's.

When Miss Ayrshire finished her first group of songs, her audience expressed its approval positively, but guardedly. She smiled bewitchingly upon the people in front, glanced up at the balconies, and then turned to the company huddled on the stage behind her. After her gay and careless bows, she retreated toward the stage door. As she passed McKann, she again brushed lightly against him, and this time she paused long enough to glance down at him and murmur, "Pardon!"

In the moment her bright, curious eyes rested upon him, McKann seemed to see himself as if she were holding a mirror up before him. He beheld himself a heavy, solid figure, unsuitably clad for the time and place, with a florid, square face, well-visored with good living and sane opinions—an inexpressive countenance. Not a rock face, exactly, but a kind of pressed-brick-and-cement face, a "business" face upon which years and feelings had made no mark—in which cocktails might eventually blast out a few hollows. He had never seen himself so distinctly in the shaving-glass as he did in that instant when Kitty Ayrshire's liquid eye held him, when her bright, inquiring glance roamed over his person. After her prehensile train curled over his boot and she was gone, his wife turned to him and said in the tone of approbation one uses when an infant manifests its groping intelligence, "Very gracious of her, I'm sure!" Mrs. Post nodded oracularly. McKann grunted.

Kitty began her second number, a group of romantic German songs which were altogether more her affair than her first number. When she turned once to acknowledge the applause behind her, she caught McKann in the act of yawning behind his hand—he of course wore no gloves—and he thought she frowned a little. This did not embarrass him; it somehow made him feel important. When she retired after the second part of the program, she again looked him over curiously as she passed, and she took marked precaution that her dress did not touch him. Mrs. Post and his wife again commented upon her consideration.

The final number was made up of modern French songs which Kitty sang enchantingly, and at last her frigid public was thoroughly aroused. While she was coming back again and again to smile and curtsy, McKann whispered to his wife that if there were to be encores he had better make a dash for his train.

"Not at all," put in Mrs. Post. "Kitty is going on the same train. She sings in *Faust* at the opera tomorrow night, so she'll take no chances."

McKann once more told himself how sorry he felt for Post. At last Miss Ayrshire returned, escorted by her accompanist, and gave the people what she of course knew they wanted: the most popular aria from the French opera of which the title-role had become synonymous with her name—an opera written for her and to her and round her, by the veteran French composer who adored her—the last and not the palest flash of his creative fire. This brought her audience all the way. They clamored for more of it, but she was not to be coerced. She had been unyielding through storms to which this was a summer breeze. She came on once more, shrugged her shoulders, blew them a kiss, and was gone. Her last smile was for that uncomfortable part of her audience seated behind her, and she looked with recognition at McKann and his ladies as she nodded goodnight to the wooden chairs.

McKann hurried his charges into the foyer by the nearest exit and put them into his motor. Then he went over to the Schenley to have a glass of beer and a rarebit before train-time. He had not, he admitted to himself, been so bored as he pretended. The minx herself was well enough, but it was absurd in his fellow-townsmen to look owlish and uplifted about her. He had no rooted dislike for pretty women; he even didn't deny that gay girls had their place in the world, but they ought to be kept in their place. He was born a Presbyterian, just as he was born a McKann. He sat in his pew in the First Church every Sunday, and he never missed a presbytery meeting when he was in town. His religion was not very spiritual, certainly, but it was substantial and concrete, made up of good, hard convictions and opinions. It had something to do with citizenship, with whom one ought to marry, with the coal business (in which his own name was powerful), with the Republican party, and with all majorities and established precedents. He was hostile to fads, to enthu-

A Gold Slipper

siasms, to individualism, to all changes except in mining machinery and in methods of transportation.

His equanimity restored by his lunch at the Schenley, McKann lit a big cigar, got into his taxi, and bowled off through the sleet.

There was not a sound to be heard or a light to be seen. The ice glittered on the pavement and on the naked trees. No restless feet were abroad. At eleven o'clock the rows of small, comfortable houses looked as empty of the troublesome bubble of life as the Allegheny cemetery itself. Suddenly the cab stopped, and McKann thrust his head out of the window. A woman was standing in the middle of the street addressing his driver in a tone of excitement. Over against the curb a lone electric stood despondent in the storm. The young woman, her cloak blowing about her, turned from the driver to McKann himself, speaking rapidly and somewhat incoherently.

"Could you not be so kind as to help us? It is Mees Ayrshire, the singer. The juice is gone out and we cannot move. We must get to the station. Mademoiselle cannot miss the train; she sings tomorrow night in New York. It is very important. Could you not take us to the station at East Liberty?"

McKann opened the door. "That's all right, but you'll have to hurry. It's 11:10 now. You've only got fifteen minutes to make the train. Tell her to come along."

The maid drew back and looked up at him in amazement. "But, the hand-luggage to carry, and Mademoiselle to walk! The street is like glass!"

McKann threw away his cigar and followed her. He stood silent by the door of the derelict, while the maid explained that she had found help. The driver had gone off somewhere to telephone for a car. Miss Ayrshire seemed not at all apprehensive; she had not doubted that a rescuer would be forthcoming. She moved deliberately; out of a whirl of skirts she thrust one fur-topped shoe—McKann saw the flash of the gold stocking above it—and alighted.

"So kind of you! So fortunate for us!" she murmured. One hand she placed upon his sleeve, and in the other she carried an armful of roses that had been sent up to the concert stage. The petals showered upon the sooty, sleety pavement as she picked her way along. They would be lying there tomorrow morning, and the children in those houses would wonder if there had been a funeral. The maid followed with two leather bags. As soon as he had lifted Kitty into his cab she exclaimed:

"My jewel-case! I have forgotten it. It is on the back seat, please. I am so careless!"

He dashed back, ran his hand along the cushions, and discovered a small leather bag. When he returned he found the maid and the luggage bestowed on the front seat, and a place left for him on the back seat beside Kitty and her flowers.

"Shall we be taking you far out of your way?" she asked sweetly. "I haven't an idea where the station is. I'm not even sure about the name. Céline thinks it is East Liberty, but I think it is West Liberty. An odd name, anyway. It is a Bohemian quarter, perhaps? A district where the law relaxes a trifle?"

McKann replied grimly that he didn't think the name referred to that kind of liberty.

"So much the better," sighed Kitty. "I am a Californian; that's the only part of America I know very well, and out there, when we called a place Liberty Hill or Liberty Hollow—well, we meant it. You will excuse me if I'm uncommunicative, won't you? I must not talk in this raw air. My throat is sensitive after a long program." She lay back in her corner and closed her eyes.

When the cab rolled down the incline at East Liberty station, the New York express was whistling in. A porter opened the door. McKann sprang out, gave him a claim check and his Pullman ticket, and told him to get his bag at the check-stand and rush it on that train.

Miss Ayrshire, having gathered up her flowers, put out her hand to take his arm. "Why, it's you!" she exclaimed, as she saw his face in the light. "What a coincidence!" She made no further move to alight, but sat smiling as if she had just seated herself in a drawing-room and were ready for talk and a cup of tea.

McKann caught her arm. "You must hurry, Miss Ayrshire, if you mean to catch the train. It stops here only a moment. Can you run?"

A Gold Slipper

"Can I run!" she laughed. "Try me!"

As they raced through the tunnel and up the inside stairway, McKann admitted that he had never before made a dash with feet so quick and sure stepping out beside him. The white-furred boots chased each other like lambs at play, the gold stockings flashed like the spokes of a bicycle wheel in the sun. They reached the door of Miss Ayrshire's state-room just as the train began to pull out. McKann was ashamed of the way he was panting, for Kitty's breathing was as soft and regular as when she was reclining on the back seat of his taxi. It had somehow run in his head that all these stage women were a poor lot physically—unsound, overfed creatures, like canaries that are kept in a cage and stuffed with song-restorer. He retreated to escape her thanks. "Good night! Pleasant journey! Pleasant dreams!" With a friendly nod in Kitty's direction he closed the door behind him.

He was somewhat surprised to find his own bag, his Pullman ticket in the strap, on the seat just outside Kitty's door. But there was nothing strange about it. He had got the last section of the train, No. 13, next to the drawing-room. Every other berth in the car was made up. He was just starting to look for the porter when the door of the state-room opened and Kitty Ayrshire came out. She seated herself carelessly in the front seat beside his bag.

"Please talk to me a little," she said coaxingly. "I'm always wakeful after I sing, and I have to hunt someone to talk to. Céline and I get so tired of each other. We can speak very low, and we shall not disturb anyone." She crossed her feet and rested her elbow on his Gladstone. Though she still wore her gold slippers and stockings, she did not, he thanked Heaven, have on her concert gown, but a very demure black velvet with some sort of pearl trimming about the neck. "Wasn't it funny," she proceeded, "that it happened to be you who picked me up? I wanted a word with you, anyway."

McKann smiled in a way that meant he wasn't being taken in. "Did you? We are not very old acquaintances."

"No, perhaps not. But you disapproved tonight, and I thought I was singing very well. You are very critical in such matters?"

He had been standing, but now he sat down. "My dear young lady, I am not critical at all. I know nothing about 'such matters.'"

"And care less?" she said for him. "Well, then we know where we are, in so far as that is concerned. What did displease you? My gown, perhaps? It may seem a little *outré* here, but it's the sort of thing all the imaginative designers abroad are doing. You like the English sort of concert gown better?"

"About gowns," said McKann, "I know even less than about music. If I looked uncomfortable, it was probably because I was uncomfortable. The seats were bad and the lights were annoying."

Kitty looked up with solicitude. "I was sorry they sold those seats. I don't like to make people uncomfortable in any way. Did the lights give you a headache? They are very trying. They burn one's eyes out in the end, I believe." She paused and waved the porter away with a smile as he came toward them. Half-clad Pittsburghers were tramping up and down the aisle, casting sidelong glances at McKann and his companion. "How much better they look with all their clothes on," she murmured. Then, turning directly to McKann again: "I saw you were not well seated, but I felt something quite hostile and personal. You were displeased with me. Doubtless many people are, but I seldom get an opportunity to question them. It would be nice if you took the trouble to tell me why you were displeased."

She spoke frankly, pleasantly, without a shadow of challenge or hauteur. She did not seem to be angling for compliments. McKann settled himself in his seat. He thought he would try her out. She had come for it, and he would let her have it. He found, however, that it was harder to formulate the grounds of his disapproval than he would have supposed. Now that he sat face to face with her, now that she was leaning against his bag, he had no wish to hurt her.

"I'm a hard-headed business man," he said evasively, "and I don't much believe in any of you fluffy-ruffles people. I have a sort of natural distrust of them all, the men more than the women."

A Gold Slipper

She looked thoughtful. "Artists, you mean?" drawing her words slowly. "What is your business?"

"Coal."

"I don't feel any natural distrust of business men, and I know ever so many. I don't know any coal-men, but I think I could become very much interested in coal. Am I larger-minded than you?"

McKann laughed. "I don't think you know when you are interested or when you are not. I don't believe you know what it feels like to be really interested. There is so much fake about your profession. It's an affectation on both sides. I know a great many of the people who went to hear you tonight, and I know that most of them neither know nor care anything about music. They imagine they do, because it's supposed to be the proper thing."

Kitty sat upright and looked interested. She was certainly a lovely creature—the only one of her tribe he had ever seen that he would cross the street to see again. Those were remarkable eyes she had—curious, penetrating, restless, somewhat impudent, but not at all dulled by self-conceit.

"But isn't that so in everything?" she cried. "How many of your clerks are honest because of a fine, individual sense of honor? They are honest because it is the accepted rule of good conduct in business. Do you know"—she looked at him squarely—"I thought you would have something quite definite to say to me; but this is funny-paper stuff, the sort of objection I'd expect from your office-boy."

"Then you don't think it silly for a lot of people to get together and pretend to enjoy something they know nothing about?"

"Of course I think it silly, but that's the way God made audiences. Don't people go to church in exactly the same way? If there were a spiritual-pressure test-machine at the door, I suspect not many of you would get to your pews."

"How do you know I go to church?"

She shrugged her shoulders. "Oh, people with these old, ready-made opinions usually go to church. But you can't evade me like that." She tapped the edge of his seat with the toe of her gold slipper. "You sat there all evening, glaring at me as if you could eat me alive. Now I give you the chance to state your objections, and you merely criticize my audience. What is it? Is it merely that you happen to dislike my personality? In that case, of course, I won't press you."

"No," McKann frowned, "I perhaps dislike your professional personality. As I told you, I have a natural distrust of your variety."

"Natural, I wonder?" Kitty murmured. "I don't see why you should naturally dislike singers any more than I dislike coal-men. I don't classify people by their occupation. Doubtless I should find some coal-men repulsive, and you may find some singers so. But I have reason to believe that, at least, I'm one of the less repellent."

"I don't doubt it," McKann laughed, "and you're a shrewd woman to boot. But you are, all of you, according to my standards, light people. You're brilliant, some of you, but you've no depth."

Kitty seemed to assent, with a dive of her girlish head. "Well, it's a merit in some things to be heavy, and in others to be light. Some things are meant to go deep, and others to go high. Do you want all the women in the world to be profound?"

"You are all," he went on steadily, watching her with indulgence, "fed on hectic emotions. You are pampered. You don't help to carry the burdens of the world. You are self-indulgent and appetent."

"Yes, I am." she assented with a candor which he did not expect. "Not all artists are, but I am. Why not? If I could once get a convincing statement as to why I should not be self-indulgent, I might change my ways. As for the burdens of the world—" Kitty rested her chin on her clasped hands and looked thoughtful. "One should give pleasure to others. My dear sir, granting that the great majority of people can't enjoy anything very keenly, you'll admit that I give pleasure to many more people than you do. One should help others who are less fortunate; at present I am supporting just eight people, besides those I hire. There was never

A Gold Slipper

another family in California that had so many cripples and hard-luckers as that into which I had the honor to be born. The only ones who could take care of themselves were ruined by the San Francisco earthquake some time ago. One should make personal sacrifices. I do; I give money and time and effort to talented students. Oh, I give something much more than that! something that you probably have never given to anyone. I give, to the really gifted ones, my *wish*, my desire, my light, if I have any; and that, Mr. Worldly Wiseman, is like giving one's blood! It's the kind of thing you prudent people never give. That is what was in the box of precious ointment." Kitty drew off her fervor with a slight gesture, as if it were a scarf, and leaned back, tucking her slipper up on the edge of his seat. "If you saw the houses I keep up," she sighed, "and the people I employ, and the motor-cars I run— And, after all, I've only this to do it with." She indicated her slender person, which Marshall could almost have broken in two with his bare hands.

She was, he thought, very much like any other charming woman, except that she was more so. Her familiarity was natural and simple. She was at ease because she was not afraid of him or herself, or of certain half-clad acquaintances of his who had been wandering up and down the car oftener than was necessary. Well, he was not afraid, either.

Kitty put her arms over her head and sighed again, feeling the smooth part in her black hair. Her head was small—capable of great agitation, like a bird's; or of great resignation, like a nun's. "I can't see why I shouldn't be self-indulgent, when I indulge others. I can't understand your equivocal scheme of ethics. Now I can understand Count Tolstoy's, perfectly. I had a long talk with him once, about his book 'What is Art?' As nearly as I could get it, he believes that we are a race who can exist only by gratifying appetites; the appetites are evil, and the existence they carry on is evil. We were always sad, he says, without knowing why; even in the Stone Age. In some miraculous way a divine ideal was disclosed to us, directly at variance with our appetites. It gave us a new craving, which we could only satisfy by starving all other hungers in us. Happiness lies in ceasing to be and to cause being, because the thing revealed to us is dearer than any existence our appetites can ever get for us. I can understand that. It something one often feels in art. It is even the subject of the greatest of all operas, which, because I can never hope to sing it, I love more than all the others." Kitty pulled herself up. "Perhaps you agree with Tolstoy?" she added languidly.

"No; I think he's a crank," said McKann, cheerfully.

"What do you mean by a crank?"

"I mean an extremist."

Kitty laughed. "Weighty word! You'll always have a world full of people who keep to the golden mean. Why bother yourself about me and Tolstoy?"

"I don't, except when you bother me."

"Poor man! It's true this isn't your fault. Still, you did provoke it by glaring at me. Why did you go to the concert?"

"I was dragged."

"I might have known!" she chuckled, and shook her head. "No, you don't give me any good reasons. Your morality seems to me the compromise of cowardice, apologetic and sneaking. When righteousness becomes alive and burning, you hate it as much as you do beauty. You want a little of each in your life, perhaps—adulterated, sterilized, with the sting taken out. It's true enough they are both fearsome things when they get loose in the world; they don't, often."

McKann hated tall talk. "My views on women," he said slowly, "are simple."

"Doubtless," Kitty responded dryly, "but are they consistent? Do you apply them to your stenographers as well as to me? I take it for granted you have unmarried stenographers. Their position, economically, is the same as mine."

McKann studied the toe of her shoe. "With a woman, everything comes back to one thing." His manner was judicial.

She laughed indulgently. "So we are getting down to brass tacks, eh? I have beaten you in argument, and now you are leading trumps."

She put her hands behind her head and her lips parted in a half-yawn. "Does everything

A Gold Slipper

come back to one thing? I wish I knew! It's more than likely that, under the same conditions, I should have been very like your stenographers—if they are good ones. Whatever I was, I would have been a good one. I think people are very much alike. You are more different than anyone I have met for some time, but I know that there are a great many more at home like you. And even you—I believe there is a real creature down under these custom-made prejudices that save you the trouble of thinking. If you and I were shipwrecked on a desert island, I have no doubt that we would come to a simple and natural understanding. I'm neither a coward nor a shirk. You would find, if you had to undertake any enterprise of danger or difficulty with a woman, that there are several qualifications quite as important as the one to which you doubtless refer."

McKann felt nervously for his watch-chain. "Of course," he brought out, "I am not laying down any generalizations—" His brows wrinkled.

"Oh, aren't you?" murmured Kitty. "Then I totally misunderstood. But remember"—holding up a finger—"it is you, not I, who are afraid to pursue this subject further. Now, I'll tell you something." She leaned forward and clasped her slim, white hands about her velvet knee. "I am as much a victim of these ineradicable prejudices as you. Your stenographer seems to you a better sort. Well, she does to me. Just because her life is, presumably, greyer than mine, she seems better. My mind tells me that dullness, and a mediocre order of ability, and poverty, are not in themselves admirable things. Yet in my heart I always feel that the sales-women in shops and the working girls in factories are more meritorious than I. Many of them, with my opportunities, would be more selfish than I am. Some of them, with their own opportunities, are more selfish. Yet I make this sentimental genuflection before the nun and the charwoman. Tell me, haven't you any weakness? Isn't there any foolish natural thing that unbends you a trifle and makes you feel gay?"

"I like to go fishing."

"To see how many fish you can catch?"

"No, I like the woods and the weather. I like to play a fish and work hard for him. I like the pussy-willows and the cold; and the sky, whether it's blue or grey—night coming on, every thing about it."

He spoke devoutly, and Kitty watched him through half-closed eyes. "And you like to feel that there are light-minded girls like me, who only care about the inside of shops and the-aters and hotels, eh? You amuse me, you and your fish! But I musn't keep you any longer. Haven't I given you every opportunity to state your case against me? I thought you would have more to say for yourself. Do you know, I believe it's not a case you have at all, but a grudge. I believe you are envious; that you'd like to be a tenor, and a perfect lady-killer!" She rose, smiling, and paused with her hand on the door of her state-room. "Anyhow, thank you for a pleasant evening. And, by the way, dream of me tonight, and not of either of those ladies who sat beside you. It does not matter much whom we live with in this world, but it matters a great deal whom we dream of." She noticed his bricky flush. "You are very naive, after all, but, oh, so cautious! You are naturally afraid of everything new, just as I naturally want to try everything: new people, new religions—new miseries, even. If only there were more new things— If only you were really new! I might learn something. I'm like the Queen of Sheba—I'm not above learning. But you, my friend, would be afraid to try a new shaving soap. It isn't gravitation that holds the world in place; it's the lazy, obese cowardice of the people on it. All the same"—taking his hand and smiling encouragingly—"I'm going to haunt you a little. *Adios!*"

When Kitty entered her state-room, Céline, in her dressing-gown, was nodding by the window.

"Mademoiselle found the fat gentleman interesting?" she asked. "It is nearly one."

"Negatively interesting. His kind always say the same thing. If I could find one really intel-ligent man who held his views, I should adopt them."

"Monsieur did not look like an original," murmured Céline, as she began to take down her lady's hair.

✢ ✢ ✢

A Gold Slipper

McKann slept heavily, as usual, and the porter had to shake him in the morning. He sat up in his berth, and after composing his hair with his fingers, began to hunt about for his clothes. As he put up the window-blind some bright object in the little hammock over his bed caught the sunlight and glittered. He stared and picked up a delicately turned gold slipper.

"Minx! hussy!" he ejaculated. "All that tall talk—! Probably got it from some man who hangs about; learned it off like a parrot. Did she poke this in here herself last night, or did she send that sneak-faced Frenchwoman? I like her nerve!" He wondered whether he might have been breathing audibly when the intruder thrust her head between his curtains. He was conscious that he did not look a Prince Charming in his sleep. He dressed as fast as he could, and, when he was ready to go to the wash-room, glared at the slipper. If the porter should start to make up his berth in his absence— He caught the slipper, wrapped it in his pajama jacket, and thrust it into his bag. He escaped from the train without seeing his tormentor again.

Later McKann threw the slipper into the wastebasket in his room at the Knickerbocker, but the chambermaid, seeing that it was new and mateless, thought there must be a mistake, and placed it in his clothes-closet. He found it there when he returned from the theater that evening. Considerably mellowed by food and drink and cheerful company, he took the slipper in his hand and decided to keep it as a reminder that absurd things could happen to people of the most clocklike deportment. When he got back to Pittsburgh, he stuck it in a lock-box in his vault, safe from prying clerks.

McKann has been ill for five years now, poor fellow! He still goes to the office, because it is the only place that interests him, but his partners do most of the work, and his clerks find him sadly changed—"morbid," they call his state of mind. He has had the pine-trees in his yard cut down because they remind him of cemeteries. On Sundays or holidays, when the office is empty, and he takes his will or his insurance-policies out of his lock-box, he often puts the tarnished gold slipper on his desk and looks at it. Somehow it suggests life to his tired mind, as his pine-trees suggested death—life and youth. When he drops over some day, his executors will be puzzled by the slipper.

As for Kitty Ayrshire, she has played so many jokes, practical and impractical, since then, that she has long ago forgotten the night when she threw away a slipper to be a thorn in the side of a just man.

Two Letters

Enrico Caruso

In his own words.

MY ONLY SWEETEST DORO:

Here I am after the performance of *Aïda* which was really triumph. There were some unive-ness but we finished the performance very well. I will describe you how everything goes.

Today was a beautiful day with the sunshine terribly hot. We beginning the performance and at moment to go on the stage this was illuminated plenety by the sun. I had like a shower of rays in my eyes terribly hot. Like Swedish bath. Then I was forced to close my eyes and impossible to look the condocter. The basso, worse than a bad corist, beginning to sing, with a voice like an old dog, doing "WHAU WHAU!!" Both things made me nervous and I beginning to sing "Celeste Aïda" with my eyes closed and a bag of sunshine on my face. Impossible to sing well and my aria was sang without feeling and for a chance I dont make a terrible *crak* before the end. I finisched well and had a good applause. But the public understand that I was no satysfide and I think himself was the same because the ovation was not enthuiastic. The second scene was same thing and there was not enthusiasm even that I sang very well. Somebody told me that the cause was the basso.

The scene of the triumph passed. Then came the scene of the Nilo [Nile]. I mounted myself and taked my public. There were many calls and people were crazy. I dont know the exact words to express what the public doit. Heats, umbrellas, hendekacifs, canes all in the aria, and a shouts that arrived in heaven. I think many people will have no voice for many days.

I must give my soul to take the public.

I will leave you for tomorrow.

You will excuse me, yes? Thanks.

All my love with all my soul.

Yours

RICO

HOTEL SEVILLA HAVANA CUBA

Monday May 31 1920 1:30 A.M.

MY DEAREST DORO SWEETHEART:

. . . I went to the theater and show your cable to Bracale. He was nearly fainting down. He told me that he will come to New York with me and implore you to accept the proposition because, he said, we cannot throw out for the window two hundred thousand dollars. I try my best to calm him, and I think now he is calm and put his soul in peace.

Then I went in my dressing-room to prepare myself for "Pagliacci." I was so nervous that you cannot imagine. But what a "Pagliacci" I sung! Surprised myself and everybody was crazy! I never see people crying like in such performance.

Two Letters

Verdi
Refunds

Giuseppe Verdi and
Prospero Bertani

What do you do if you don't like the new opera by Verdi? Get your money back from the composer, of course.

To Giuseppe Verdi

On the second of this month, attracted by the sensation which your opera, *Aïda*, was making I went to Parma. Half an hour before the performance began I was already in my seat, No. 120. I admired the scenery, listened with great pleasure to the excellent singers, and took pains to let nothing escape me. After the performance was over, I asked myself whether I was satisfied. The answer was in the negative. I returned to Reggio and on the way back in the railroad carriage, I listened to the verdicts of my fellow travelers. Nearly all of them agreed that *Aïda* was a work of the highest rank.

Thereupon I conceived a desire to hear it again, and so on the fourth I returned to Parma. I made the most desperate efforts to obtain a reserved seat, and there was such a crowd that I had to spend five lire to see the performance in comfort.

I came to the following conclusion: the opera contains absolutely nothing thrilling or electrifying, and if it were not for the magnificent scenery, the audience would not sit through it to the end. It will fill the theater a few more times and then gather dust in the archives. Now, my dear Signor Verdi, you can imagine my regret at having spent 32 lire for these two performances. Add to this the aggravating circumstance that I am dependent on my family, and you will understand that this money preys on my mind like a terrible specter. Therefore I address myself frankly and openly to you, so that you may send me this sum. Here is the account:

Railroad: one way	2.60 lire
Railroad: return trip	3.30 "
Theater	8.00 "
Disgustingly bad dinner at the station	2.00 "
	15.90 lire
	x 2 "
	31.80 lire

In the hope that you will extricate me from this dilemma, I am yours sincerely,

BERTANI

My address: Bertani, Prospero; Via San Domenico, No.5

May, 1872

VERDI'S REPLY (ADDRESSED TO RICCORDI)

. . . As you may readily imagine, in order to save this scion of his family from the specters that pursue him, I shall gladly pay the little bill he sends me. Be so kind, therefore, as to have one of your agents send the sum of 27 lire, 80 centesimi to this Signor Prospero Bertani, Via San Domenico, No. 5. True, that isn't the whole sum he demands, but for me to pay for his

Verdi Refunds

dinner too would be wearing the joke a bit thin. He could perfectly well have eaten at home. Naturally, he must send you a receipt, as well as a written declaration that he promises never to hear another one of my new operas, so that he won't expose himself again to the danger of being pursued by specters, and that he may spare me further travel expenses!

May 15, 1872

I, the undersigned, certify herewith that I have received the sum of 27.80 lire from Maestro Giuseppe Verdi, as reimbursement of my expenses for a trip to Parma to hear the opera, *Aida*. The Maestro felt it was fair that this sum should be restored to me, since I did not find his opera to my taste. At the same time, it is agreed that I shall undertake no trip to hear any of the Maestro's new operas in the future, unless he takes all the expenses upon himself, whatever my opinion of his work may be.

In confirmation whereof I have affixed my signature,

BERTANI PROSPERO

ACADEMY of MUSIC
14th-st.
UNION SQUARE

MR. HACKETT, whilst assuring the public that the nightly cost of the entertainment offered them here, exceeds by six times that of the most expensive of either of the other places of amusement in the city, is desirous and in the hope of affording the patrons of the OPERA every reasonable satisfaction, proposes, during the limited engagement here of MADAME GRISI and SIGNOR MARIO, the following graduate scale of

PRICES OF ADMISSION:

ENTRANCE TICKET TO PARQUETTE AND FIRST
CIRCLE OF BOXES.....................................TWO DOLLARS
Check for a secured seat, One Dollar Additional.
SECOND CIRCLE OF BOXES................................ONE DOLLAR
Where the seats may be occupied by the audience respectively according to the order of their entrance.
AMPHITHEATRE...FIFTY CENTS
PRIVATE & PROSCENIUM BOXES, according to locality
and capacity, from...$5 to $30 each

THIRD NIGHT
OF MADAME
GRISI
And SIGNOR
MARIO

FRIDAY, OCTOB'R 6th
Will be performed, Bellini's Tragic Opera of
NORMA

NORMA	MADAME GRISI
Adalgisa	Signorina Donovani
POLLIO	SIGNOR MARIO
Oroveso	Signor Susini
Clotilda	Signora Morra
Flavio	Signor Patti
Musical Director and Conductor	Signor Arditi

Doors open at half-past 6, Opera to commence at half-past 7.

Tickets and places can be secured daily at the Box Office on Irving Place from 8 A. M., till 5 P. M., and also at William Hall & Son's, 239 Broadway, and at VanNorden & King's, 45 Wall-street.

CARRIAGES will set down in Irving Place from Fourteenth-street, and take up in reverse order. The Third and Fourth Avenue Cars, and Bowery and Broadway stages all set down passengers near the Academy.

The Wagnerians

Louis Auchincloss

In a New York clan of impeccable lineage, the black sheep finds momentary redemption as manager of the Metropolitan Opera— and in the process gives his family a memorable lesson in the differences between art and life.

Dear Mr. Styles:

When I told you that I would not "write up" Uncle Ed for your history of opera in the Americas, you implied that I was being stuffy. Privately I have no doubt that you used a harsher word. "What bad luck," you must have said to your fellow editors, "that the only person living who remembers Edmund Stillman should be a prudish niece who is determined to take her sixty-year secrets with her virginity to the grave!" Oh, yes, I can imagine how you young writers talk. I have not always led the cloistered existence of the New York old maid, bounded on the south by Carnegie Hall and on the north by the Colony Club. No, Mr. Styles, you will be surprised to hear that I had an operatic career of my own! I sang in public—on one occasion.

And that is precisely why I have now revised (not changed) my position. I have decided that my reluctance to write about Uncle Ed must spring from my identification of his failure as manager of the opera house with my own failure as an opera singer. What egotism! To compare his magnificent and catastrophic experiment with ten years of voice lessons ending in a single appearance as Ortrud in a road company *Lohengrin*! And so I have resolved that I will do what you ask and record here my memories of my uncle. But, there is one very stiff condition. You may not publish it in my lifetime. For even though these memories are so ancient that they have ceased to hurt, there are still some that I do not care to see set forth in the impertinence of print: the quizzical, puzzled stare in Uncle Ed's eyes after too many brandies, my father's embarrassment before the devoted ushers at the opera house, who he feared were his brother's unpaid creditors, my grandmother's bewilderment at finding herself choosing to side with her own world against her favorite son. But when I am gone (and I am past eighty), you may do as you like with these pages. They will be in nobody's memory then.

I shall start, being old-fashioned, in the time-honored way of Balzac (the only novelist I still read), by saying a word about the position of the Stillmans in the New York of 1890. We were one of those unremarkable families, indigenous to the "best" society of any large city, who seemed to have no particular claim to our position other than the fact that we had always had it. By a claim I mean such an obvious thing as a fortune or a distinguished lineage or simply a relationship to some great man. There are New York families that have their colonial governor as Roman families have their Pope. But each generation of our Stillmans had managed to move gracefully across the social scene without particularly distinguishing itself or particularly disgracing itself and always without leaving more than a modest competence to the succeeding one. They were great believers in the "here and now." So long as their dinners were good and their clothes in style, they did not much care what sort of old brownstone (provided, of course, it was in the right neighborhood) housed them. They found the world as it was a pretty good place. Of course, they didn't go around turning over stones or poking behind curtains. They did not conceive that to be their function. But if a curtain happened to fall and a skeleton was revealed, if a moral issue developed and people started to raise their voices and take sides, if, in other words, the chips were down, the Stillmans, God bless them, were apt to be on the side of the angels.

Uncle Ed, my father's bachelor brother, was the Stillman who came closest to breaking the

The Wagnerians

family rule of "Nothing in Excess," but his excess was of a Stillman sort. In personal adornment he was a bit of a peacock, even in that gaudy age. Look at the photograph of him in Gustav Kobbe's *Complete Opera Book*. The long slim body in the perfectly tailored Prince Albert with the velvet collar seems to flow gracefully upward to the grave bearded face, the reflective eyes and the glistening, narrow-brimmed stovepipe hat. The beard is neatly trimmed to follow the contours of the squarish chin and also those of the gently drooping mustache. It would be altogether the portrait of a dandy of the period, with a bit of the hardness of a one of Whistler's *boulevardiers*, a touch of the cruelty of a Paul Borget hero, were it not for the eyes, large and brown and almost brooding. Oh, yes, the eyes gave Uncle Ed away as they gave my father away. They were eyes that could see the main chance, but beyond the main chance they saw perfectly the price that one paid for it.

A more serious excess in Uncle Ed was his drinking, but this, too, was done with Stillman style. There was never (at least before his final European chapter) anything so vulgar as intoxication. Uncle Ed, as Father used to put it, was like a noble greensward that needed a constant, gentle sprinkling. Each drink had its consecrated hour: the mid-morning sherry flip, the noon gin fizz, the afternoon cognac, the evening "cocktail" at the men's bar, the midnight whiskey, without mentioning the diverse flow of mealtime wines that constituted the central river to which the other drinks were tributary. The family used to ascribe Uncle Ed's drinking to his lack of steady employment, and from my earliest years I remember table discussion of how to lure him from his bibulous idleness. Uncle Ed, apparently, was always willing to try anything once, but his jobs had a way of terminating after a few months, always with the remarkable circumstance of his remaining a fast friend of his former employer.

It was my father who first conceived the idea of finding him a job at the opera house. Father was always the most imaginative member of the family. Physically, he resembled his brother, but it was as a guinea fowl resembles a pheasant. Father was much less elegant and, by like token, much more responsible. But he had the kindness of the Stillman men, and when he put his mind on his brother, he thought of his brother and not of himself thinking of his brother.

"Everybody wants Ed to do what *they* happen to like doing," he told my grandmother, above whose sober widow's establishment Uncle Ed maintained a bachelor's top floor. "Uncle Harry wants him to go into the iron business. My boss keeps urging him to become a banker. And Marion Crawford tells him to write novels. We ought to be trying to make a life for Ed out of the things that *Ed* likes doing. Now what are they? Well, first off, he likes the opera. Couldn't Uncle Harry get him something to do there?"

It was the ace of trumps on the first draw! Granny Stillman's older sister, my Great-Aunt Rosalie, was married to Uncle Harry Belknap, a rich ironmaster from Troy and a director of the opera. Nothing was easier for him than to secure for his wife's nephew, whom most of the boxholders knew and liked, the position of secretary to the company, and for the next two years (an unprecedented tenure for him) Uncle Ed attended the board meetings faithfully and ornamentally, kept the minutes neatly and concisely and busied himself about the office, at least until the early afternoon. He even took to dropping in on rehearsals, and with his knack for friendship he soon became intimate with the leading singers and musicians. The opera house developed for him into a combination of hobby and club, and my family breathed in relief at Father's brilliant solution of the problem.

Promotion followed swiftly. In those days the gulf between the owners of the opera house, all New York businessmen, and the artists, already dominated by Germans and Wagnerites, was almost unbridgeable. Neither side could even listen to the other, and opera was produced in an atmosphere of what we would call a "cold war." But Uncle Ed could talk to Mr. Morgan and to Mr. Damrosch and make each feel that he was on his side. When the general managership fell vacant in 1890, the board, after several long, wrangling sessions, was suddenly united by the prospect of this dark but very glossy horse.

There was an outburst of enthusiasm. What did it matter that Ed Stillman was not a musician? Was there not too much expertise already? Were the directors not sick of managers who

The Wagnerians

swore guttural oaths and regarded "opera" and "Wagner" as synonyms? The only trouble seemed to be with Uncle Ed himself, who resisted the appointment with a stubbornness that surprised everybody, and, when at last prevailed upon, accepted it with a gravity of manner that seemed almost Teutonic. Had the directors paused, however, to remember how the miter had changed Thomas à Becket (which, needless to say, they did not), they might have consoled themselves with the thought that they were twelve King Henrys to his single archbishop.

One person who had no reservations over Uncle Ed's promotion was his sixteen-year-old niece. I was already a devoted opera fan, with a picture by my bedside of Melba, whose London debut as Lucia had been the great moment of my life. I attended the Brearly School, but books, and even, in holiday parties, boys, hardly existed for me. I lived for the afternoons and my singing teacher, Miss Angela Frith. Uncle Ed, whose courteous demeanor to the young raised them briefly to the paradise of adults, was already my favorite relative. Now he became a god.

Mother, who considered herself vastly more liberal than the Stillmans, was as one with them when it came to any serious extension of the arts beyond the parlor. She laughed at my musical pretensions, when she was not irritated by them.

"Why don't you take Amy to one of your rehearsals, Ed?" she asked my uncle one night. "I wonder if seeing the opera house in its shirtsleeves wouldn't cure some of her fancies?"

Poor Mother! If she only had known what oil she was pouring on my fire! I waited breathless for Uncle Ed's answer, afraid to ruin my chances by showing my enthusiasm, but his smile recognized my palpitations. He knew that waiting was torture to the young.

"Why, certainly, any rehearsal she wants. We're running through the second act of *Tristan* tomorrow afternoon. How will that do?"

And so, after a sleepless night and a morning at school in which I took in nothing, my dream came true. There was I, Amy Stillman, seated with my uncle in the center of the second row of the orchestra pit in the great dark, empty opera house before a stage covered with cartons and dirty canvases, watching two stout middle-aged persons, a man and a woman in modern dress, sitting side by side on a small wicker divan. And when the conductor raised his baton, and we started right off in the middle of the love duet, I thought it the most romantic setting that I had ever seen. So much for Mother's precautions!

I was familiar with *Lohengrin* and *Die Walküre*, but I had never heard a note of *Tristan*. Its effect on me was ambivalent. I was intrigued and excited by the violence and the surge of the music, but at the same time it made me restless, apprehensive, almost afraid. Of what? Of love, of physical love? I have often asked myself since. But I do not think so. It was difficult for a girl in my time to associate love with the portly middle age represented by the two performers. No, there was something else in that churning, seething music, something like being caught in the backwash of a big breaker when surf bathing in Southampton on a visit to Granny, tossed and pulled by the hissing water and borne out ineluctably to sea, to be smothered, perhaps to be drowned in a terrible peace beneath that tormented surface. I had no idea that this was a common reaction to *Tristan*, and I became at length so agitated that I was relieved when the music director called to the conductor through a little megaphone to stop the music.

The woman who was singing Brangäne had been delivering the off-stage warning in a voice that was almost inaudible. She complained that the strain on her vocal cords was so great that she could not sing in full voice until the performance. It could be then or now, she concluded defiantly. The *Herr Direktor* could choose. The latter turned to Uncle Ed.

"Which shall it be, Mr. Stillman?"

"Tell her to sing today," Uncle Ed snapped, and the rehearsal went on. Inexperienced as I was, I could sense that he had already taken hold of his company.

In a break, after the duet, Uncle Ed suggested a turn around the block. I was very proud to be on the arm of my handsome and distinguished uncle, and I admired the easy courtesy with which he raised his hat to any members of the company whom we passed, without interrupting the flow of our discussion. He asked me which I preferred, *Tristan* or *Lucia*, already knowing that *Lucia* was my favorite opera.

The Wagnerians

"Oh, *Lucia*," I said promptly. "But *Tristan* is more interesting," I added politely, suspecting his own preference.

"Interesting," he repeated thoughtfully. "Perhaps that's just what it is. Look down Broadway, Amy." We paused at the corner and gazed south at the great thoroughfare. "Look at all that gray dirtiness and listen to all that strident clamor and tell me if you really think our modern life corresponds to the tinkling tunefulness of Donizetti."

"You believe it should?"

"Well, don't you think there should be *some* relation between daily life and music? Or do we go to the opera just to dress up and see our friends?"

"But Uncle Ed," I protested earnestly, "shouldn't opera help us to forget all that dirt and clamor?"

"Spoken like a true boxholder! You'll be just like the other dreamers in Number Seven, Amy. Your grandmother sighs for Edgar of Ravenswood, and even your Great-Aunt Rosalie wants to immolate herself with Rhadames in a living tomb!"

"And I can be Carmen!" I exclaimed, feeling very adult to be joking about such things (particularly Granny!) with the older generation.

"I'm sure a very proper Carmen," Uncle Ed added with a chuckle. "Maybe even a rather severe one, like dear Lili Lehmann. She sings the 'Habañera' as if it had been written by Haydn. I suppose, Amy, I sometimes feel that our life is such a continual fancy dress ball that I want—just for a minute, mind you, just every now and then—to slip into plain old clothes and be myself."

As I took in with a quick glance my uncle's rich brown tweeds, the maroon polish of his shoes gleaming beneath his spats, the red carnation in his buttonhole, the walking stick with the silver knob, I could not but wonder if *these* were his plain old clothes. "Does your *Tristan* 'correspond' to modern life?" I asked timidly.

Uncle Ed became immediately serious at this, more so than I could ever remember having seen him. "That's a good question, Amy. No, Wagner's operas don't correspond to modern life because Wagner didn't believe in modern life. Not in ours, anyway. He thought that it didn't exist, or if it did, that it was too trivial, too unheroic, too sordid, to be worth commenting on in musical terms. If a man was to write opera, it should be about valiant mythological figures, gods and goddesses, and if there weren't any gods and goddesses, he ought to create them. Think of it, Amy!" Here Uncle Ed's eyes really sparkled. We stopped walking, and he spread one arm in a broad gesture. "Ever since Shakespeare we have taken for granted that the artist must deal with mortal men, that his province must lie in love and compassion. You remember what Pope said: the proper study of mankind is man. But Wagner did what nobody has done in the whole history of art, except perhaps the ancients. If he was compelled to comment, he would create a world worthy to comment upon. He despised mankind, but did that stop him? He saw that the only beautiful thing in the world was death, and he made love to it in *Tristan*. Oh, Amy, when once you *feel* Wagner, there is nobody else. There is nothing else."

How vivid that moment is to me this day, more than sixty years after! For I saw things then that were beyond the comprehension of my years in a terrible flash of divination. It was not that I agreed with Uncle Ed. I didn't then, and, thank God, I do not now. But I *saw*, and the vision scared me. I saw into the awful emptiness of his soul, and I felt the well of pity bubbling up in my own. Because, you see, Mr. Styles, I felt that I had seen into something essential in the nature of my family, or at least of the Stillman side of it, something that Granny had all along suspected and that she fought blindly, without understanding. And this was it: Uncle Ed's elegance, his smartness, his whole air of exquisite maintenance, was the same gallant but essentially futile effort to decorate the void of God's or non-God's neglect that he fancied he could detect in the tumultuous creations of Wagner. It all had to end, as it ended in *Tristan*, in a death that one could only pretend was a love death.

My shudder was barely perceptible, but Uncle Ed perceived it. He shook his head, apologized for his theorizing (always, in his opinion, "bad form") and led me back to the opera house. "If Granny Stillman hears I've been trying to convert you to Wagner, there'll be the

The Wagnerians

devil to pay," he said with a wink, as we took our seats. "If she asks you what was being rehearsed today, tell her it was *Les Huguenots*."

Granny, of course, had not been born a Stillman, and she had none of their characteristics. She was a good deal tougher and less imaginative, and she was much more innately conservative. Where Father and Uncle Ed were by temperament aristocratic, she was bourgeois to the marrow of her bones. She had been widowed early in life and had managed her small inheritance so well that she was now able to maintain a house on Sixty-fifth Street and a shingle cottage in Southampton and to keep a butler and four maids. But always frugal, she depended on her richer sister for the luxuries of a carriage and an opera box.

I look at Granny's photograph as I write, with the pale oval face, the high-piled, elaborately waved gray hair and the large, watery, apprehensive eyes, and I think how she would stare at the liberties I am taking with her! Yet I have started this thing, and I have to make her understandable. Granny believed in the present, the present instant, the concrete thing before her eyes. Having said she was bourgeois, I will now say that she had a bit of the peasant in her. She accepted the mores of her New York as if established by divine decree. When her favorite niece lay dying, we were all surprised that she seemed wholly concerned with whether of not to call off a dinner party. But this was not from lack of feeling. It was from a deep-seated belief that doing the "right thing" was paramount to personal grief, and it gave an oddly impersonal quality to her snobbishness. She never scorned outcasts, any more than, conventionally anti-Semitic and anti-Roman, she in the least disliked or disapproved of Jews or Catholics. She simply would not pick her friends among them.

I believe that Granny loved Uncle Ed more than she had ever loved another human being (unless it was the rather shadowy figure of my long-dead grandfather), but when rumors began to circulate that he had "gone over to the Germans" and even that he had "betrayed his trust," she found herself in an acutely painful position. She and her sister, Aunt Rosalie Belknap, were close with the peculiar closeness of their generation of siblings: they lived on the same street in Manhattan and on the same sand dune in Southampton and saw each other every day of the year. Aunt Rosalie, being older and cleverer and a great deal richer, dominated Granny, while Uncle Harry, who took care of her business interests, represented "men" in her respectful widow's heart. If the Belknaps were against the "new music," how could a Stillman be for it? How much less could a Stillman be for it who owed his very job to Uncle Harry?

Matters came to a head on the Sunday after that rehearsal, at Granny's family lunch. As in other brownstones of that period, the dining room was the one handsome chamber, always on the first floor back, shrouded in kindly darkness, high-ceilinged, with perfectly polished silver gleaming in crowded density on the sideboard and with high, carved Jacobean chairs looking like antiques under the crystal chandelier. When I inherited Granny's and put them in a good light, they showed up as bad fakes.

Aunt Rosalie, as was to be expected, led off the discussion. To tell the truth, I always found Aunt Rosalie, who dyed her hair a jet black and wore too many rings and bracelets, the least bit common, whereas Granny, even at her most worldly, was always totally a lady. Money sometimes had that effect on old New York. Granny may have owed her relative refinement to her relative poverty.

"They tell me young Damrosch is twisting you around his little finger, Ed," Aunt Rosalie began. "They say we're going to have nothing but darkened stages with earth goddesses moaning about time and fate."

"Oh, I think I can promise you a Rhine maiden here and there, Aunt Rosalie," Uncle Ed drawled in his easiest tone. "And we've installed some very curious machinery to make them appear to be swimming about under water. I think it might interest you to see it. Would you care to come down to the house one morning next week and let me show you?"

Uncle Ed could have his way with most women, even with Aunt Rosalie, but not when she was on the track of something. "It'll have to wait, I'm afraid, for I'm tied up all next week. But Harry and I would like very much to know what you're planning to tell your board when they find that all their lovely Traviatas and Aïdas have been traded in for a parcel of shriek-ing Valkyries. Wouldn't we, Harry?"

"Very much, my dear."

"Ah, but I'm all ready for the board, Uncle Harry, I assure you," Uncle Ed exclaimed, turn-ing deferentially to the old white-whiskered gentleman. "I have ordered a new dragon for *Siegfried*, and you can't even object to the expense, as I've raised the money myself. It is guar-anteed to send shivers down the hardiest spine. Fire and smoke come out of its jaws, and its eyes goggle hideously. I predict that even you, Uncle Harry, won't sleep through that scene!"

Uncle Harry grunted, and I giggled and Mother smiled, but there was a distinct feeling at the table that Uncle Ed was going rather far. Granny did not attempt to conceal her apprehension.

"I don't think that's very polite to your uncle, Edmund," she intervened, as if he were five and not forty-five. "After all, it was he who suggested your name originally to the board. He is going to bear the responsibility for what you do. *He* is going to be the one to face the box-holders!"

"I know that, Ma! I couldn't be more aware of it. But the day is also coming when Uncle Harry will be proud to have made me the manager. He will be known in musical history as the man responsible for the first all-star Wagner performances in this country!"

Uncle Harry looked so uncomfortable at this that even Aunt Rosalie saw that the conver-sation had better be changed, and we turned to the happier topic of who could be dropped that year from her ever-expanding Christmas party.

The struggle between Uncle Ed and the boxholders came to its crisis during a Monday night performance of *Tristan und Isolde* with the same cast that I had seen rehearsing it. I sat as usual on family parties in the front row of the Belknap box between Aunt Rosalie, who always occupied her special armchair on the left, and Granny. It was a trying seat, for I had to sit up as straight as they did. Aunt Rosalie even had a little cushion, as hard as a board, which hung down over the back rest to keep her from tilting. But what was far worse than the strain of the posture, at least to a music lover like myself, was the way, with a license as broad as their physical freedom was narrow, they exchanged comments about the opera across me in perfectly normal speaking tones.

In the second row were my parents and Miss Behn, one of those soft, chattering, semi-indigent old maids, always smiling, always looking to the "bright side" of their faintly illuminated existences, who attached themselves to the Aunt Rosalies of that era as pilot fish to sharks. And alone in a corner at the back of the box, a nodding Jupiter, Uncle Harry slept the sleep of the just fiduciary.

Why did they go to the opera? What took them, *every* Monday night, year in and year out? Could it have been only snobbery, as people believe today. I would be the last to deny that snobbery played its part, but it seems to me that there had to be something else, something deeper in the folkways of human communities. Monday night at the opera was like a village fair or a saint's festival. Society was still small enough so that one knew, if not everybody, at least who everybody was, and who were their guests and why. Many young people today do not know what this pleasure is. The impersonality of the modern city has destroyed it. But in New York you can still see a strange atavistic yearning for something not unlike it in the Easter Parade. What used to be a leisurely stroll of familiar figures in new finery down Fifth Avenue after church has become a turgid human river, overflowing the sidewalks and filling the thoroughfare to the elimination of all vehicles, a dense, slowly moving mass without origin or destination, drawn from the desolate suburbs, thousands upon thousands of women in silly hats, staring and being stared at, recognizing nobody and ignorant of why they are there, zombies seeking a lost ritual of community living that they will never find. Thank God my life has been largely lived in another day.

We arrived very late that night, to my distress but hardly to my surprise. Tristan and Isolde were already drinking the potion, and Granny and Aunt Rosalie were sufficiently diverted by the shouts of the sailor chorus so that no real ennui had settled in before the long entr'acte. In the second act, the love duet held everyone's attention, but trouble came, after the inter-

The Wagnerians

ruption of the lovers, with King Mark's long aria. The ripple of conversation through the boxes swelled to a gurgling stream.

I had done my homework on *Tristan* since the rehearsal, and I remember thinking that it was ironical that Granny and Aunt Rosalie's world should be most bored when Wagner was speaking most directly to them. For Mark sings of the day, which in *Tristan* is always compared unfavorably to the night. The day is reality: it is harsh and bright and garish. It is full of things that boxholders like to talk about: honor, loyalty, ties of blood. But the night, which to the lovers has become the only truth, is dark and lush and sleep-inducing. The night is death and love.

The chatter in the boxes reached a pitch that I had not heard before. It was actually difficult to catch some of Mark's notes. Suddenly, appallingly, silence fell with the unexpected downward swoop of the great curtains, the music stopped, and the lights went up. A tall bearded gentleman in white tie and tail coat strode quickly across the proscenium and faced the audience across the prompter's box. It was Uncle Ed. His high tense voice rang out in the auditorium.

"When the boxholders have concluded their conversations, the performance will be resumed. That is all. Thank you."

And he walked offstage as rapidly as he had come on. There was a moment of shocked silence, then a buzz of startled whispers, then some whistles and finally the roar of resumed conversation and a stamping of feet. The boxholders consulted each other indignantly; there were shrill complaints and some laughs. From the galleries came catcalls that might have expressed anger at the interruption or approval of the management. One could not be sure of anything in the general confusion.

In the midst of it all Uncle Ed appeared again, but this time in the back of our box where he took a seat beside Uncle Harry, for once thoroughly awake. Uncle Ed tilted his chair back and crossed his arms over his chest in the gesture of one who was prepared to wait all night. In a minute the entire diamond horseshoe was aware of his presence there. The issue was joined.

I am sure that that was the most terrible moment of Granny's long life. I had heard of her near insanity at the early death of my apparently charming grandfather, and I was later to minister to her in her desolation at the death of each of her two sons. But there is a compensation in the very fullness of the tide of love that creates the agony of bereavement; there is the luxury of memory always open to us. No such leavening existed that night for Granny. She could not even console herself that her most beloved child was showing an admirable courage in his isolation. It is always difficult for the conventional to recognize courage in what they deem ridiculous causes. Here was Granny, surrounded by the only world that she knew and admired, in the very heart of it and at its dressiest moment, and having to behold it united in an anger and contempt, which to her, alas, was a *justifiable* anger and contempt, by the perverse, misguided son who sat behind her with folded arms and icy countenance, identifying her and her family and her sister with his foolish fads. It was as if a respectable Roman matron, on a holiday matinee at the Colosseum, should have had the shock of seeing a son leap into the arena to shield some dirty Christian from a hungry and deserving lion. Granny's discipline was of the tautest, but I could see her jaw tremble as it only did in moments of the very gravest tension. Then, without turning to me, she touched my elbow.

"Ask your uncle to have the performance resumed," she murmured, as I leaned over to her. "Tell him I say: 'please.'"

It was in our family a lady's SOS, the ultimate appeal. I stepped to the back of the box, terrified to think that the eyes of the multitude were upon me, and whispered the message hastily in his ear. He nodded gravely, and in the second that I caught his eyes I read in them all of his gallantry and all of his defeat. He rose and left the box, and in five more minutes the curtain rose again, before a still chattering house, on the garden by King Mark's castle. It was then that I grew up—in a single minute—and felt at last the full tragedy of what had happened.

✣ ✣ ✣

The Wagnerians

Only two days later Father gave us the news at breakfast of the Uncle Ed's resignation.

"I'm afraid it's a case of 'I quit,' 'you're fired,'" he said with a sad headshake. "He's going abroad almost at once. Your grandmother is terribly upset, Amy, and she finds it easier on her nerves not to be left alone with him. I think you'd better take the day off from school and spend it with her."

"But why is it hard for her to be alone with Uncle Ed?"

Father and Mother exchanged glances, and then he abandoned the subterfuge. "Well, I guess you're old enough to hear about it. Your uncle has run up some very serious debts, and he will find it cheaper and more convenient to live in Germany while arrangements are being made about them. Your grandmother can't afford to dig any deeper into her capital than she's already done, and she's afraid that he will try to persuade her."

I do not know if it was the restraint of my presence, but Uncle Ed certainly made no remark during lunch at Granny's that could even remotely be construed as referring to his financial exigency. Indeed, anyone watching the three of us in that dusky, silent dining room would have assumed that Granny was the one harassed by creditors. For all the reputed discipline of her generation, she made not the slightest effort at conversation, but simply sat there staring with tear-filled eyes at the errant son who was holding forth gracefully to me about the reasons for the popular failure of German opera.

"Haven't we heard enough about that sorry business?"

"Very well, Ma."

"I don't see how you can be so cold, so casual."

"I don't see how you can be so flurried, so emotional!"

"Edmund!" Granny cried. "I can't bear it! You know, my dear, that I would give you what you ask if it was fair to the others. . . ."

"I know, Ma. Of course. Please! Remember Amy."

After lunch, when Granny had gone to her room for a nap (nothing ever interrupted that), Uncle Ed followed me down the hall and helped me into my coat. It was a long red coat with some twenty buttons down the front, and in my nervousness and distress, I buttoned one in the wrong hole. Uncle Ed turned me to face him and carefully unbuttoned it to button it again properly.

"It doesn't matter," I murmured. "I'm only going home, just a block."

Uncle Ed raised a reproachful finger. "It always matters, Amy. Remember that. It *always* matters. Those are the only words of wisdom—the only assets, in fact—that your departing uncle leaves behind."

And then, like Granny, I too broke down. I threw my arms around his neck and sobbed.

"Poor Amy," he said, stroking my hair, "life is going to be hard on you, too. Just remember what I told you about the buttons. It doesn't sound like much, and it's *not* much, but it may be better than nothing. If it's all you've got."

I ran out the door and down the stoop, and I never saw him again.

Three years later, when I was in Paris with Father and Mother, they went to see him at his hotel, but they would not let me go with them. By then he was intoxicated most of the time, and in a few more months his liver mercifully gave out.

My own story is only a sad postscript to Uncle Ed's. Without his example I might have faced the fact earlier that I did not have a voice for Wagnerian opera and reconciled myself to marriage and children. But the idea of a Stillman carrying on where he had failed became a fixation. I even believed that I owed it to him to sing the great roles as gloriously as he had dreamed of hearing them. Had Mother and Father ever divined this madness, they might have helped me, but it was part of my crazy integrity to tell them nothing.

After graduating from Brearly School, I refused adamantly to "come out," and I opposed my mother and grandmother so violently in every other plan which they proposed for me, that Father, always the peacemaker, at last had to take charge of the situation. He decreed that I should be allowed to study the voice under professional auspices. Of course, it went without saying that I should continue to live at home, but I was permitted to spend my mornings in the studio of Madame Grisi-Helsinka, to be ostensibly trained to appear in benefit per-

The Wagnerians

formances on the concert stage. Of course, *I* was determined that I would make my debut as Sieglinde, but there was no need to throw it in my family's face until the time arrived.

My teacher scoffed at my Wagnerian pretensions and tried to turn me to operetta. My voice, such as it was, turned out to be nearer contralto than soprano. But there was still Fricka, Erda, Ortrud to be sung. I persisted in my lessons. For ten years I studied German opera, the same decade that witnessed the great popular triumph of Wagner in New York that Uncle Ed had predicted. The irony of my situation and the endless queries of my family drove me at last abroad, where, at the age of thirty, I sang Ortrud for a road company in Rouen, my debut and my finale.

For a cable came, not of congratulation but of recall. Granny was ill. She had had a stroke, which I was made to feel was not unrelated to the absurdity of my operatic career. Father had at the same time come down with a kidney disease that was to kill him, and as Mother had to spend all her time with him, she insisted that my place was with Granny. I debated my reply for a desperate week, and in the end I decided that Mother was right. I sailed home from Le Havre and spent seven dreary years with Granny until her death at the age of ninety-one. By then I was thirty-seven, and there was no further question of an appearance in opera. The family had won—or thought they had.

But I must insist on one point. Everybody has always taken for granted that I was talked into looking after first Granny and later Mother. They say: "Poor old Amy. She wanted to have her little fling, you know, but old Mrs. Stillman put a stop to all that. They preferred to have her a useful 'companion' to an indifferent opera singer." Everybody assumes that I was simply another of those weak-minded spinsters of the late Victorian era who bowed their heads submissively as they were cheated of their birthrights by selfish mothers and grandmothers. But is wasn't so. It cannot have been so! What I did, I did under nobody's persuasion but my own. I took a long clear look at my opera career and weighed it against what I could do for Granny. Had I had the voice for Isolde I hope that I would have had the divine egotism and the courage to let Granny die alone. As it was, I could not sacrifice the small consolation that I was able to bring her for the chance to sing second-string roles in third-rate opera companies.

But we had our moments, Uncle Ed and I. Who knows, as Robert Browning might have put it, when all is finally added up, if we will not have had as much as the others? It is more graceful, anyway, to think so. It is like keeping that twentieth button properly buttoned on one's coat. And so I am going to be glad for what I have had. I am going to be glad for my little night in Rouen, and I wonder if Uncle Ed, even in those sorry last years, was not occasionally glad that he had had the thrill of producing *Tristan*, if only to a golden horseshoe of chattering friends and relations.

Sincerely yours,
AMY STILLMAN

The Wagnerians

Il Janitoro

George Ade

Even the most devoted aficionado will admit that opera's excesses can sometimes be just a bit much. Humorist George Ade brings us back to earth.

M r. Tyler paid $7 for two opera tickets

Although he slept through one duet he felt fully repaid for going because Mrs. Tyler raved over the opera and wasted all her superlatives on it. The music was "heavenly," the prima donna "superb" and the tenor "magnificent."

There is nothing so irritates a real enthusiast as the presence of calm scorn.

"Don't you like it?" asked Mrs. Tyler, as she settled back after the eighth recall of the motherly woman who had been singing the part of a sixteen-year-old maiden.

"Oh, yes; it's all right," replied Mr. Tyler, as if he were conceding something.

"All right! Oh, you iceberg! I don't believe you'd become enthusiastic over anything in the world."

"I like the music my dear, but the grand opera drags so. Then the situations are so preposterous they always appeal to my sense of humor. I can't help it. When I see Romeo and Juliet die, both singing away as if they enjoyed it, I have to laugh."

"The idea!"

"You take it in this last act. Those two fellows came out with the soldiers and announced that they were conspiring and didn't want to be heard by the people in the house, and then they shouted in chorus until they could have been heard two miles away."

"Oh, you are prejudiced."

"Not at all. I'll tell you, a grand opera's the funniest kind of show if you only take the right view of it."

Thus they argued, and even after they arrived home she taunted him and told him he could not appreciate the dignity of the situations.

It was this nagging which induced Mr. Tyler to write an act of grand opera. He chose for his subject an alarm of fire in an apartment house. He wanted something modern and up-to-date, but for his method of treatment he resolved to reverently follow all the traditions of grand opera. The act, hitherto unpublished, and written solely for the benefit of Mrs. Tyler, is here appended:

(MR. AND MRS. TAYLOR *are seated in their apartment on the fifth floor of a Behemoth residential flat building.* MRS. TAYLOR *arises, places her hand on her heart, and moves to the center of the room.* MR. TAYLOR *follows her, with his right arm extended.*)

MRS. TAYLOR: I think I smell smoke.

MR. TAYLOR: She thinks she smells smoke.

MRS. TAYLOR: I think I smell smoke.

MR. TAYLOR: Oh. What is it? She says she thinks she smells smoke.

MRS. TAYLOR: What does it mean, what does it mean?

 This smell of smoke may indicate,

 That we'll be burned—oh-h-h, awful fate!

MR. TAYLOR: Behold the smell grows stronger yet,

 The house is burning, I'd regret

 To perish in the curling flames;

 Oh, horror! horror! horror!!!

MR. AND MRS. TAYLOR: Oh, sad is our lot, sad is our lot,

Il Janitoro

To perish in the flames so hot,
To curl and writhe and fry and sizz
Oh, what a dreadful thing it is
To think of such a thing!

MRS. TAYLOR: We must escape!

MR. TAYLOR: Yes, yes, we must escape!

MRS. TAYLOR: We have no time to lose.

MR. TAYLOR: Ah, bitter truth, Ah, bitter truth,
We have no time to lose.

MR. AND MRS. TAYLOR: Sad is our lot, sad is our lot,
To perish in the flames so hot.

MR. TAYLOR: Hark, what is it?

MRS. TAYLOR: Hark, what is it?

MR. TAYLOR: It is the dread alarm of fire.

MRS. TAYLOR: Ah, yes, ah, yes, it is the dread alarm.

MR. TAYLOR: The dread alarm strikes on the ear
And chills me with an awful fear.
The house will burn, oh, can it be
That I must die in misery,
That I must die in misery,
The house will burn, oh, can it be
That I must die in misery?

MRS. TAYLOR: Come, let us fly!

MR. TAYLOR: 'Tis well. 'Tis well. We'll fly at once.
(*Enter all the other residents of the fifth floor*)

MR. TAYLOR: Kind friends, I have some news to tell.
This house is burning; it were well

George Ade   ❈ 144 ❈

That we should haste ourselves away
And save our lives without delay.

CHORUS: What is this he tells us?
It must be so;
The building is on fire
And we must go.
Oh, hasten, oh, hasten, oh, hasten away.
Our terror we should not conceal,
And language fails to express the alarm
That in our hearts we feel.

MR. AND MRS. TAYLOR: Oh, language fails to express the alarm
That in their hearts they feel.

(*Enter the* JANITOR)

JANITOR: Hold, I am here.

MR. TAYLOR: Ah, it is the Janitoro.

MRS. TAYLOR: Can I believe my senses,
Or am I going mad?
It is the Janitoro,
It is indeed the Janitoro

JANITOR: Such news I have to tell.

MR. TAYLOR: Ah, I might have known
He has such news to tell.
Speak and break the awful suspense.

MRS. TAYLOR: Yes, speak.

JANITOR: I come to inform you
That you must quickly fly
The fearful blaze is spreading,

Il Janitoro

To tarry is to die.
The floors underneath you
Are completely burned away.
They cannot save the building,
So now escape I pray.

MRS. TAYLOR: Oh, awful message.
How it chills my heart.

JANITOR: The flames are roaring loudly,
Oh, what a fearful sound!
You can hear the people shrieking
As they jump and strike the ground.
Oh, horror overtakes me,
And I merely pause to say
That the building's doomed for certain
Oh, haste, oh, haste away.

MRS. TAYLOR: Oh, awful message.
How it chills my heart.
Yet we will sing a few more arias
Before we start.

MR. TAYLOR: Yes, a few more arias and then away.

CHORUS: Oh, hasten, oh, hasten, oh, hasten away.

MRS. TAYLOR: Now, e'er I retreat,
Lest death o'ertakes me
I'll speak of the fear
That convulses and shakes me,
I sicken to think what may befall,
Oh, horror! horror!! horror!!

George Ade

MR. TAYLOR: The woman speaks the truth,
And there can be no doubt
That we will perish soon
Unless we all clear out.
CHORUS: Oh, hasten, oh hasten, oh hasten away!

(But why go further? The supposition is that they continued the dilatory tactics of grand opera and perished in the flames.)

The Voice of the Turtle

W. Somerset Maugham

Maugham is asking which is worse, the shamelessly shallow diva or the naive young writer who idolizes her. And then comes that voice, "mellow and crystalline"...

For some time I could not make up my mind if I liked Peter Melrose or not. He had had a novel published that had caused some stir among the rather dreary but worthy people who are always on the lookout for new talent. Elderly gentlemen with nothing much to do but go to luncheon parties praised it with girlish enthusiasm, and wiry little women who didn't get on with their husbands thought it showed promise. I read a few reviews. They contradicted one another freely. Some of the critics claimed that with this first novel the author had sprung into the front rank of English novelists: others reviled it. I did not read it. I have learnt by experience that when a book makes a sensation it is just as well to wait a year before you read it. It is astonishing how many books then you need not read at all. But it chanced that one day I met Peter Melrose. With some misgiving I had accepted an invitation to a sherry party. It was in the top flat of a converted house in Bloomsbury, and I was a trifle out of breath when I had climbed four flights of stairs. My hostesses were two women, much over-lifesize, in early middle life, the sort of women who know all about the insides of motor cars and like a good tramp in the rain, but very feminine for all that, fond of eating out of paper bags. The drawing room, which they called "our workshop," though being of independent means neither had ever done a stroke of work in her life, was large and bare, furnished with rustless-steel chairs, which looked as though they could with difficulty support the very substantial weight of their owners, glass-topped tables and a vast divan covered with zebra skin. On the walls were bookshelves, and pictures by the better-known English imitators of Cézanne, Braque and Picasso. In the shelves, besides a number of "curious" books of the eighteenth century (for pornography is ageless) there were only the works of living authors, mostly first editions, and it was indeed to sign some of my own that I had been asked to the party.

It was quite small. There was but one other woman, who might have been a younger sister of my hostesses, for, though stout, she was not quite so stout, though tall, not quite so tall, and though hearty, not quite so hearty. I did not catch her name, but she answered to that of Boofuls. The only man besides myself was Peter Melrose. He was quite young, twenty-two or twenty-three, of the middle height, but with an ungainly figure that made him look squat. He had a reddish skin that seemed to fit over the bones of his face too tightly, a rather large Semitic nose, though he was not a Jew, and alert green eyes under bushy eyebrows. His brown hair, cut very short, was scurfy. He was dressed in the brown Norfolk jacket and grey flannel trousers that are worn by the art students who wander hatless along King's Road, Chelsea. An uncouth young man. Nor was there much to attract in his manner. He was self-assertive, disputatious and intolerant. He had a hearty contempt for his fellow writers which he expressed with zest. The satisfaction he gave me by his breezy attacks on reputations which for my part I considered exaggerated, but prudently held my tongue about, was only lessened by the conviction that no sooner would my back be turned than he would tear my own to shreds. He talked well. He was amusing and sometimes witty. I should have laughed at his sallies more easily if those three ladies had not been so unreasonably convulsed by them. They roared with laughter at what he said, whether it was funny or whether it was inept. He said many silly things, for he talked without stopping, but he also said some very clever ones. He had a point of view, crude and not so original as he thought, but sincere. But the most striking thing about him was his eager, impetuous vitality; it was like a hot flame that burnt him with an unendurable fury. It even shed a glow on those about him. He had something, if only that, and when I left it was with a slight sense of curiosity at what would come of him. I did not know if he had talent; so many young things can write a clever novel—that means nothing; but it seemed to me that as a man he was not quite like everybody else. He was the sort of person who at thirty, when time had softened his asperity and experience had taught him that he was not quite so intelligent as he thought, would turn into an interesting and agreeable fellow. But I never expected to see him again.

It was with surprise that I received two or three days later a copy of his novel with a very flattering dedication. I read it. It was obviously autobiographical. The scene was a small town in Sussex, and the characters of the upper middle class that strives to keep up appearances on an inadequate income. The humor was rather brutal and rather vulgar. It grated on me, for it consisted chiefly of mockery at people because they were old and poor. Peter Melrose did not know how hard those misfortunes are to bear, and that the efforts made to cope with them are more deserving of sympathy than of derision. But there were descriptions of places, little pictures of a room or impressions of a countryside, which were excellently done. They showed tenderness and a sense of the spiritual beauty of material things. The book was written easily, without affectation, and with a pleasant feeling for the sound of words. But what made it indeed somewhat remarkable, so that I understood why it had attracted attention, was the passion that quivered in the love story of which the plot, such as it was, consisted. It was, as is the modern fashion, more than a trifle coarse and, again in the modern fashion, it tailed off vaguely, without any particular result, so that everything was left in the end pretty much as it had been in the beginning; but you did get the impression of young love, idealistic and yet vehemently sexual; it was so vivid and so deeply felt that it took your breath away. It seemed to throb on the printed page like the pulse of life. It had no reticence. It was absurd, scandalous and beautiful. It was like a force of nature. That was passion all right. There is nothing, anywhere, so moving and so awe-inspiring.

W. Somerset Maugham   ❧ 152 ❧

I wrote to Peter Melrose and told him what I thought of his book, then suggested that we might lunch together. He rang me up the next day, and we made a date.

I found him unaccountably shy when we sat down opposite one another at a table in a restaurant. I gave him a cocktail. He talked glibly enough, but I could not help seeing that he was ill at ease. I gained the impression that his self-assurance was a pose assumed to conceal, from himself maybe, a diffidence that tortured him. His manners were brusque and awkward. He would say a rude thing and then laugh nervously to cover his own embarrassment. Though he pretended to be so sure of himself, he wanted all the time to be reassured by you. By irritating you, by saying the things he thought would annoy, he tried to force from you some admission, tacit it might be, that he was as wonderful as he longed to think himself. He wanted to despise the opinion of his fellows, and nothing was more important to him. I thought him rather an odious young man, but I did not mind that. It is very natural that clever young men should be rather odious. They are conscious of gifts that they do not know how to use. They are exasperated with the world that will not recognize their merit. They have something to give, and no hand is stretched out to receive it. They are impatient for the fame they regard as their due. No, I do not mind odious young men; it is when they are charming that I button up the pockets of my sympathy.

Peter Melrose was extremely modest about his book. He blushed though his reddish skin when I praised what I liked in it, and accepted my strictures with a humility that was almost embarrassing. He had made very little money out of it, and his publishers were giving him a small monthly allowance in advance of royalties on the next one. This he had just started, but he wanted to get away to write it in peace, and knowing I lived on the Riviera he asked me if I could tell him of a quiet place where he could bathe and live cheaply. I suggested that he should come and spend a few days with me so that he could look about till he found something to suit him. His green eyes sparkled when I proposed this, and he flushed.

"Shouldn't I be an awful nuisance?"

The Voice of the Turtle

"No. I shall be working. All I can offer you is three meals a day and a room to sleep in. It'll be very dull, but you can do exactly what you like."

"It sounds grand. May I let you know if I decide to come?"

"Of course."

We separated, and a week or two later I went home. This was in May. Early in June I received a letter from Peter Melrose asking, if I had really meant what I said when I invited him to spend a few days with me, whether he might arrive on such and such a date. Well, at the time I had meant it, but now, a month later, I remembered that he was an arrogant and ill-bred youth, whom I had seen but twice and wasn't in the least interested in, and I didn't mean it any longer. It seemed to me very likely that he would be bored stiff. I lived a very quiet life and saw few people. And I thought it would be a great strain on my nerves if he were as rude as I knew he could be and I as his host felt it behooved me to keep my temper. I saw myself driven beyond endurance and ringing the bell to have his clothes packed and the car brought round to take him away within half an hour. But there was nothing to do about it. It would save him the cost of board and lodging to spend a short period with me, and if he was tired and unhappy, as he said in his letter, it might be that it would do him good. I sent him a wire, and shortly afterwards he arrived.

He looked very hot and grubby in his grey flannel trousers and brown tweed coat when I met him at the station, but after a swim in the pool he changed into white shorts and a Cochet shirt. He looked then quite absurdly young. He had never been out of England before. He was excited. It was touching to see his delight. He seemed, amid those unaccustomed surroundings, to lose his sense of himself, and he was simple, boyish and modest. I was agreeably surprised. In the evening, after dinner, sitting in the garden, with only the croaking of the little green frogs to break the silence, he began talking to me of his novel. It was a romantic story about a young writer and a celebrated prima donna. The theme was reminiscent of Ouida, the last thing I should have expected this hard-boiled youth to write, and I was tickled; it was odd how the fashion completed the circle and returned generation after generation to the same themes. I had no doubt that Peter Melrose would treat it in a very modern way, but there it was, the same old story as had entranced sentimental readers in three-volume novels of the eighties. He proposed to set it in the beginning of the Edwardian era, which to the young has already acquired the fantastic, far-away feeling of a past age. He talked and talked. He was not unpleasant to listen to. He had no notion that he was putting into fiction his own daydreams, the comic and touching daydreams of a rather unattractive, obscure young man who sees himself beloved, to the admiration of the whole world, by an incredibly beautiful, celebrated and magnificent woman. I always enjoyed the novels of Ouida, and Peter's idea did not at all displease me. With his charming gift of description, his vivid, ingenuous way of looking at material things, fabrics, pieces of furniture, walls, trees, flowers, and the power of representing the passion of life, the passion of love that thrilled every fiber of his own uncouth body, I had a notion that he might well produce something exuberant, absurd and poetical. But I asked him a question.

"Have you ever known a prima donna?"

"No, but I've read all the autobiographies and memoirs that I could find. I've gone into it pretty thoroughly. Not only the obvious things, you know, but I've hunted around in all sorts of byways to get the revealing touch or the suggestive anecdote."

"And have you got what you wanted?"

"I think so."

He began to describe his heroine to me. She was young and beautiful, wilful it is true and with a quick temper, but magnanimous. A woman on a grand scale. Music was her passion; there was music not only in her voice, but in her gestures and in her inmost thoughts. She was devoid of envy, and her appreciation of art was such that when another singer had done her an injury she forgave her when she heard her sing a role beautifully. She was of a wonderful generosity, and would give away everything she possessed when a story of misfortune touched her soft heart. She was a great lover, prepared to sacrifice the world for the man she

The Voice of the Turtle

loved. She was intelligent and well read. She was tender, unselfish and disinterested. In fact she was much too good to be true.

"I think you'd better meet a prima donna," I said at last.

"How can I?"

"Have you ever heard of La Falterona?"

"Of course I have. I've read her memoirs."

"She lives just along the coast. I'll ring her up and ask her to dinner."

"Will you really? It would be wonderful."

"Don't blame me if you don't find her quite what you expect."

"It's the truth I want."

Everyone has heard of La Falterona. Not even Melba had a greater reputation. She had ceased now to sing in opera, but her voice was still lovely, and she could fill a concert hall in any part of the world. She went for long tours every winter, and in summer rested in a villa by the sea. On the Riviera people are neighbors if they live thirty miles from one another, and for some years I had seen a good deal of La Falterona. She was a woman of ardent temperament, and she was celebrated not only for her singing, but for her love affairs: she never minded talking about them, and I had often sat entranced for hours while, with the humor which to me was her most astonishing characteristic, she regaled me with lurid tales of royal or very opulent adorers. I was satisfied that there was at least a measure of truth in them. She had been married, for short periods, three or four times, and in one of these unions had annexed a Neapolitan prince. Thinking that to be known as La Falterona was grander than any title, she did not use his name (to which indeed she had no right, since after divorcing him she had married somebody else); but her silver, her cutlery and her dinner service were heavily decorated with a coat of arms and a crown, and her servants invariably addressed her as *madame la princesse*. She claimed to be Hungarian, but her English was perfect, she spoke it with a slight accent (when she remembered), but with an intonation suggestive, I had been told, of Kansas City. This she explained by saying that her father was a political exile who had fled to America when she was no more than a child; but she did not seem quite sure whether he was a distinguished scientist who had got into trouble for his liberal views, or a Magyar of high rank who had brought down on his head the imperial wrath because he had had a love affair with an archduchess. It depended on whether she was just an artist among artists, or a great lady among persons of noble birth.

With me she was, not natural, for she could never have been if she had tried, but franker than with anyone else. She had a natural and healthy contempt for the arts. She genuinely looked upon the whole thing as a gigantic bluff, and deep down in her heart was an amused sympathy for all the people who were able to put it over on the public. I will admit that I looked forward to the encounter between Peter Melrose and La Falterona with a good deal of sardonic amusement.

She liked coming to dine with me because she knew the food was good. It was the only meal she ate in the day, for she took great care of her figure, but she liked that one to be succulent and ample. I asked her to come at nine, knowing that was the earliest hour she dreamt of eating, and ordered dinner for half past. She turned up at a quarter to ten. She was dressed in apple-green satin, cut very low in front, with no back at all, and she wore a string of huge pearls, a number of expensive-looking rings, and on her left arm diamond and emerald bracelets from the wrist to the elbow. Two or three of them were certainly real. On her raven black hair was a thin circlet of diamonds. She could not have looked more splendid if she had been going to a ball at Stafford House in the old days. We were in white ducks.

"How grand you are," I said. "I told you it wasn't a party."

She flashed a look of her magnificent black eyes at Peter.

"Of course it's a party. You told me your friend was a writer of talent. I am only an interpreter." She ran one finger down her flashing bracelets. "This is the homage I pay to the creative artist."

I did not utter the vulgar monosyllable that rose to my lips, but offered her what I knew was her favorite cocktail. I was privileged to call her Maria, and she always called me Master. This she did, first because she knew it made me feel a perfect fool, and secondly because, though she was in point of fact not more than two or three years younger than me, it made it quite clear that we belonged to different generations. Sometimes, however, she also called me "you dirty swine." This evening she certainly might very well have passed for thirty-five. She had those rather large features which somehow do not seem to betray age. On the stage she was a beautiful woman, and even in private life, notwithstanding her big nose, large mouth and fleshy face, a good-looking one. She wore a brown make-up, with dark rouge, and her lips were vividly scarlet. She looked very Spanish and, I suspected, felt it, for her accent at the beginning of dinner was quite Sevillian. I wanted her to talk so that Peter should get his money's worth, and I knew there was but one subject in the world that she could talk about. She was in point of fact a stupid woman who had acquired a line of glib chatter which made people on first meeting her think she was as brilliant as she looked; but it was merely a performance she gave, and you soon discovered that she not only did not know what she was talking about, but was not in the least interested in it. I do not think she had ever read a book in her life. Her knowledge of what was going on in the world was confined to what she was able to gather by looking at the pictures in the illustrated press. Her passion for music was complete bunkum. Once at a concert to which I went with her she slept all through the Fifth Symphony, and I was charmed to hear her during the interval telling people that Beethoven stirred her so much that she hesitated to come and hear him, for with those glorious themes singing through her head, it meant that she wouldn't sleep a wink all night. I could well believe she would lie awake, for she had had so sound a nap during the Symphony that it could not but interfere with her night's rest.

But there was one subject in which her interest never failed. She pursued it with indefatigable energy. No obstacle prevented her from returning to it; no chance word was so remote that she could not use it as a stepping-stone to come back to it, and in effecting this she displayed a cleverness of which one would never have thought her capable. On this subject she could be witty, vivacious, philosophic, tragic and inventive. It enabled her to exhibit all the resources of her ingenuity. There was no end to its ramifications, and no limit to its variety. This subject was herself. I gave her an opening at once, and then all I had to do was to make suitable interjections. She was in great form. We were dining on the terrace, and a full moon was obligingly shining on the sea in front of us. Nature, as though she knew what was proper to the occasion, had set just the right scene. The view was framed by two tall black cypresses, and all round us on the terrace the orange trees in full flower exhaled their heady perfume. There was no wind, and the candles on the table flamed with a steady softness. It was a light that exactly suited La Falterona. She sat between us, eating heartily and thoroughly appreciating the champagne, and she was enjoying herself. She gave the moon a glance. On the sea was a broad pathway of silver.

"How beautiful nature is," she said. "My God, the scenery one has to play in. How can they expect one to sing? You know, really, the sets at Covent Garden are a disgrace. The last time I sang Juliet I just told them I wouldn't go on unless they did something about the moon."

Peter listened to her in silence. He ate her words. She was better value than I had dared to hope. She got a little tight not only on the champagne but on her own loquaciousness. To listen to her you would have thought she was a meek and docile creature against whom the whole world was in conspiracy. Her life had been one long bitter struggle against desperate odds. Managers treated her vilely, impresarios played foul tricks on her, singers combined to ruin her, critics bought by the money of her enemies wrote scandalous things about her, lovers for whom she had sacrificed everything used her with base ingratitude; and yet, by the miracle of her genius and her quick wits, she had discomfited them all. With joyous glee, her eyes flashing, she told us how she had defeated their machinations and what disaster had befallen the wretches who had stood in her way. I wondered how she had the nerve to tell the disgraceful stories she told. Without the smallest consciousness of what she was doing she showed herself vindictive and envious, hard as nails, incredibly vain, cruel, self-

The Voice of the Turtle

ish, scheming and mercenary. I stole a glance now and then at Peter. I was tickled at the confusion he must be experiencing when he compared his ideal picture of the prima donna with the ruthless reality. She was a woman without a heart. When at last she left us, I turned to Peter with a smile.

"Well," I said, "at all events you've got some good material."

"I know, and it all fits in so beautifully," he said with enthusiasm.

"Does it?" I exclaimed, taken aback.

"She's exactly like my woman. She'll never believe that I'd sketched out the main lines of her character before I'd ever seen her."

I stared at him in amazement.

"The passion for art. The disinterestedness. She has that same nobility of soul that I saw in my mind's eye. The small-minded, the curious, the vulgar put every obstacle in her way, and she sweeps them all aside by the greatness of her purpose and the purity of her ends." He gave a little happy laugh. "Isn't it wonderful how nature copies art? I swear to you, I've got her to the life."

I was about to speak; I held my tongue; though I shrugged a spiritual shoulder, I was touched. Peter had seen in her what he was determined to see. There was something very like beauty in his illusion. In his own way he was a poet. We went to bed, and two or three days later, having found a pension to his liking, he left me.

In course of time his book appeared, and like most second novels by young people it had but a very moderate success. The critics had overpraised his first effort and now were unduly censorious. It is of course a very different thing to write a novel about yourself and the people you have known from childhood and to write one about persons of your own invention. Peter's was too long. He had allowed his gift for word painting to run away with him, the humor was still rather vulgar; but he had reconstructed the period with skill, and the romantic story had that same thrill of real passion which in his first book had so much impressed me.

After the dinner at my house I did not see La Falterona for more than a year. She went for a long tour in South America and did not come down to the Riviera till late in the summer. One night she asked me to dine with her. We were alone but for her companion-secretary, an Englishwoman, Miss Glaser by name, whom La Falterona bullied and ill treated, hit and swore at, but whom she could not do without. Miss Glaser was a haggard person of fifty, with grey hair and a sallow, wrinkled face. She was a queer creature. She knew everything there was to be known about La Falterona. She both adored and hated her. Behind her back she could be extremely funny at her expense, and the imitation she gave in secret of the great singer with her admirers was the most richly comic thing I have ever heard. But she watched over her like a mother. It was she who, sometimes by wheedling, sometimes by sheer plainness of speech, caused La Falterona to behave herself something like a human being. It was she who had written the singer's exceedingly inaccurate memoirs.

La Falterona wore pale blue satin pajamas (she liked satin) and, presumably to rest her hair, a green silk wig; except for a few rings, a pearl necklace, a couple of bracelets and a diamond brooch at her waist, she wore no jewelry. She had much to tell me of her triumphs in South America. She talked on and on. She had never been in more superb voice, and the ovations she had received were unparalleled. The concert halls were sold out for every performance, and she had made a packet.

"Is it true or is it not true, Glaser?" cried Maria with a strong South American accent.

"Most of it," said Miss Glaser.

La Falterona had the objectionable habit of addressing her companion by her surname. But it must long since have ceased to annoy the poor woman, so there was not much point in it.

"Who was that man we met in Buenos Aires?"

"Which man?"

"You fool, Glaser. You remember perfectly. The man I was married to once."

"Pepe Zapata," Miss Glaser replied without a smile.

"He was broke. He had the impudence to ask me to give him back a diamond necklace he'd given me. He said it had belonged to his mother."

"It wouldn't have hurt you to give it him," said Miss Glaser. "You never wear it."

"Give it him back?" cried La Falterona, and her astonishment was such that she spoke the purest English. "Give it him back? You're crazy."

She looked at Miss Glaser as though she expected her there and then to have an attack of acute mania. She got up from the table, for we had finished our dinner.

"Let us go outside," she said. "If I hadn't the patience of an angel I'd have sacked that woman long ago."

La Falterona and I went out, but Miss Glaser did not come with us. We sat on the veranda. There was a magnificent cedar in the garden, and its dark branches were silhouetted against the starry sky. The sea, almost at our feet, was marvelously still. Suddenly La Falterona gave a start.

"I almost forgot. Glaser, you fool," she shouted, "why didn't you remind me?" And then again to me: "I'm furious with you."

"I'm glad you didn't remember till after dinner," I answered.

"That friend of yours and his book."

I didn't immediately grasp what she was talking about.

"What friend and what book?"

"Don't be so stupid. An ugly little man with a shiny face and a bad figure. He wrote a book about me."

"Oh! Peter Melrose. But it's not about you."

"Of course it is. Do you take me for a fool? He had the impudence to send it to me."

"I hope you had the decency to acknowledge it."

"Do you think I have the time to acknowledge all the books twopenny-halfpenny authors send me? I expect Glaser wrote to him. You had no right to ask me to dinner to meet him.

I came to oblige you, because I thought you liked me for myself, I didn't know I was just being made use of. It's awful that one can't trust one's oldest friends to behave like gentlemen. I'll never dine with you again so long as I live. Never, never, never."

She was working herself into one of her tantrums, so I interrupted her before it was too late.

"Come off it, my dear," I said. "In the first place the character of the singer in that book, which I suppose is the one you're referring to—"

"You don't suppose I'm referring to the charwoman, do you?"

"Well, the character of the singer was roughed out before he'd even seen you, and besides it isn't in the least like you."

"How d'you mean, it's not like me? All my friends have recognized me. I mean, it's the most obvious portrait."

"Mary," I expostulated.

"My name is Maria, and no one knows it better than you, and if you can't call me Maria you can call me Madame Falterona or Princess."

I paid no attention to this.

"Did you read the book?"

"Of course I read it. When everyone told me it was about me."

"But the boy's heroine, the prima donna, is twenty-five."

"A woman like me is ageless."

"She's musical to her finger tips, gentle as a dove, and a miracle of unselfishness; she's frank, loyal and disinterested. Is that the opinion you have of yourself?"

"And what is *your* opinion of me?"

"Hard as nails, absolutely ruthless, a born intriguer and as self-centered as they make 'em."

She then called me a name which a lady does not habitually apply to a gentleman who, whatever his faults, has never had his legitimacy called in question. But though her eyes flashed I could see that she was not in the least angry. She accepted my description of her as complimentary.

"And what about the emerald ring? Are you going to deny that I told him that?"

The story of the emerald ring was this: La Falterona was having a passionate love affair with the Crown Prince of a powerful state, and he had made her a present of an emerald of immense value. One night they had a quarrel, high words passed, and some reference being made to the ring she tore it off her finger and flung it in the fire. The Crown Prince, being a man of thrifty habit, with a cry of consternation, threw himself on his knees and began raking out the coals till he recovered the ring. The Falterona watched him scornfully as he groveled on the floor. She didn't give much away herself, but she could not bear economy in others. She finished the story with these splendid words:

"After that I *couldn't* love him."

The incident was picturesque and had taken Peter's fancy. He had used it very neatly.

"I told you both about that in the greatest confidence and I've never told it to a soul before. It's a scandalous breach of confidence to have put it into a book. There are no excuses either for him or for you."

"But I've heard you tell the story dozens of times. And it was told me by Florence Montgomerie about herself and the Crown Prince Rudolf. It was one of her favorite stories, too. Lola Montez used to tell it about herself and the King of Bavaria. I have little doubt that Nell Gwyn told it about herself and Charles II. It's one of the oldest stories in the world."

She was taken aback, but only for an instant.

"I don't see anything strange in its having happened more than once. Everyone knows that women are passionate and that men are as mean as cat's meat. I could show you the emerald if you liked. I had to have it reset of course."

"With Lola Montez it was pearls," I said ironically. "I believe they were considerably damaged."

"Pearls?" She gave that brilliant smile of her. "Have I ever told you about Benjy Riesenbaum and the pearls? You might make a story out of it."

Benjy Riesenbaum was a person of great wealth, and it was common knowledge that for a long time he had been the Falterona's lover. In fact it was he who had bought her the luxurious little villa in which we were now sitting.

"He'd given me a very handsome string in New York. I was singing at the Metropolitan, and at the end of the season we traveled back to Europe together. You never knew him, did you?"

"No."

"Well, he wasn't bad in some ways, but he was insanely jealous. We had a row on the boat because a young Italian officer was paying me a good deal of attention. Heaven knows, I'm the easiest woman in the world to get on with, but I will not be bullied by any man. After all, I have my self-respect to think of. I told him where he got off, if you understand what I mean, and he slapped my face. On deck if you please. I don't mind telling you I was mad. I tore the string of pearls off my neck and flung it in the sea. 'They cost fifty thousand dollars,' he gasped. He went white. I drew myself up to my full height. 'I only valued them because I loved you,' I said. And I turned on my heel."

"You were a fool," I said.

"I wouldn't speak to him for twenty-four hours. At the end of that time I had him eating out of my hand. When we got to Paris the first thing he did was to go to Cartier's and buy me another just as good."

She began to giggle.

"Did you say I was a fool? I'd left the real string in the bank in New York, because I knew I was going back next season. It was an imitation one that I threw in the sea."

She started to laugh, and her laugh was rich and joyous and like a child's. That was the sort of trick that thoroughly appealed to her. She chortled with glee.

"What fools men are," she gasped. "And you, you thought I'd throw a real string into the sea."

She laughed and laughed. At last she stopped. She was excited.

"I want to sing. Glaser, play an accompaniment."

A voice came from the drawing room.

"You can't sing after all that food you walloped down."

"Shut up, you old cow. Play something, I tell you."

There was no reply, but in a moment Miss Glaser began to play the opening bars of one of Schumann's songs. It was no strain on the voice, and I guessed that Miss Glaser knew what she was doing when she chose it. La Falterona began to sing, in an undertone, but as she heard the sounds come from her lips and found that they were clear and pure, she let herself go. The song finished. There was silence. Miss Glaser had heard that La Falterona was in magnificent voice, and she sensed that she wished to sing again. The prima donna was standing in the window, with her back to the lighted room, and she looked out at the darkly shining sea. The cedar made a lovely pattern against the sky. The night was soft and balmy. Miss Glaser played a couple of bars. A cold shiver ran down my spine. La Falterona gave a little start as she recognized the music, and I felt her gather herself together.

"Mild und leise wie er lächelt
Wie das Auge hold er öffnet."

It was Isolde's death song. She had never sung in Wagner, fearing the strain on her voice, but this, I suppose, she had often sung in concerts. It did not matter now that instead of an orchestral accompaniment she had only the thin tinkle of the piano. The notes of the heavenly melody fell upon the still air and traveled over the water. In that too-romantic scene, in that lovely night, the effect was shattering. La Falterona's voice, even now, was exquisite in its quality, mellow and crystalline; and she sang with wonderful emotion, so tenderly, with such tragic, beautiful anguish that my heart melted within me. I had a most awkward lump in my throat when she finished, and looking at her I saw that tears were streaming down her face. I did not want to speak. She stood quite still, looking at that ageless sea.

W. Somerset Maugham ❧ 166 ❧

What a strange woman! I thought then that I would sooner have her as she was, with her monstrous faults, than as Peter Melrose saw her, a pattern of all the virtues. But then people blame me because I rather like people who are a little worse than is reasonable. She was hateful, of course, but she was irresistible.

Louis Melançon
METROPOLITAN OPERA
NEW YORK CITY, 1.

Italian Music in Dakota

Walt Whitman

"But for the opera," said Whitman, "I could never have written Leaves of Grass.*"*

ITALIAN MUSIC IN DAKOTA.

["*The Seventeenth—the finest Regimental Band I ever heard.*"]

Through the soft evening air enwinding all,
Rocks, woods, fort, cannon, pacing sentries, endless wilds,
In dulcet streams, in flutes' and cornets' notes,
Electric, pensive, turbulent, artificial,
(Yet strangely fitting even here, meanings unknown before,
Subtler than ever, more harmony, as if born here, related here,
Not to the city's fresco'd rooms, not to the audience of the opera house,
Sounds, echoes, wandering strains, as really here at home,
Sonnambula's innocent love, trios with *Norma's* anguish,
And thy ecstatic chorus *Poliuto*;)
Ray'd in the limpid yellow slanting sundown,
Music, Italian music in Dakota.

While Nature, sovereign of this gnarl'd realm,
Lurking in hidden barbaric grim recesses,
Acknowledging rapport however far remov'd,
(As some old root or soil of earth its last-born flower of fruit,)
Listens well pleas'd.

Acknowledgments

Selections

Excerpt from *Master Class* by Terrence McNally, copyright © 1995 by Terrence McNally. Used by permission of Dutton Signet, a division of Penguin Books USA Inc. ✤ "The Callas Cult" reprinted with the permission of Simon & Schuster from *The Queen's Throat* by Wayne Koestenbaum. Copyright © 1993 by Wayne Koestenbaum. ✤ "Death by Enthusiasm" is taken from *Murder at the Opera*, edited by Thomas Godfrey. ✤ "*Butterfly*'s Failure" reprinted with the permission of Simon & Schuster from *Puccini* by George R. Marek. Copyright © 1951 by George R. Marek, copyright renewed © 1979 by George R. Marek. ✤ Text of "Two Letters" reprinted with the permission of Simon & Schuster from *Enrico Caruso* by Dorothy Caruso. Copyright © 1945 by Dorothy Caruso, copyright renewed © 1972 by Jacqueline Ingraham Porter. ✤ "Verdi Refunds" is taken from *Verdi, the Man in His Letters*, edited by Franz Werfel. ✤ "The Wagnerians" is from *The Collected Stories of Louis Auchincloss*. Copyright © 1994 by Louis Auchincloss. Reprinted by permission of Houghton Mifflin Company. Previously published in *Tales of Manhattan* (1964, 1966, 1967). ✤ Text of "Il Janitoro" from *The Best of George Ade*. Selected and Edited by A. L. Lazarus, published by the Indiana University Press (copyright © 1985). ✤ "The Voice of the Turtle" is taken from *The Mixture as Before* by W. Somerset Maugham. Reprinted with the permission of A. P. Watt Ltd on behalf of The Royal Literary Fund.

Photographs and illustrations

Photographs on pages 76 and 114 and the illustrations on pages 56, 120, and 175 are courtesy of the Music Collection, The New York Public Library for the Performing Arts; Astor, Lenox and Tilden Foundations. ✢ Illustrations on pages 8, 90, and 170 and the poster on page 119 are courtesy of Collection of The New-York Historical Society. ✢ Photographs on frontispiece and on pages 22, 36, 110, 140, 148, and 168 are courtesy of Photofest.

Additional thanks to . . .

Larry Peterson, once again, for negotiating rights and permissions; Sue Canavan, Maria Fernandez, Donna Spillane, and Bindu Poulose for their image research; Ruth Ro and Catie O'Brien for their help with production; Morgan Entrekin for his guidance and vision; Colin Dickerman for his helpful suggestions and patience; The New York Society Library for its gracious assistance; Carla Lalli for her support; and to Jennifer Lyons.

I would like to acknowledge my debt to George Marek for the letters in "Two Letters" and "Verdi Refunds." And I would like to also thank my father, Alton, who listened to Alban Berg Saturday mornings while I was trying to watch cartoons and who therefore must share some responsibility for this book. —D.B.